# THE CHURCH LIFE MODEL

## A Biblical Pattern for the Spirit-filled Church

There's an awakening among leaders today—hear the Holy Spirit's trumpet call to all of us. Wayne Lee's book is one of the "high notes" of alert; going deeper, to lead local church teams to drink from wells meant for the church—timelessly!

—Jack W. Hayford
Chancellor, The King's University

After reading *The Church Life Model: A Biblical Pattern for the Spirit-filled Church* by Wayne and Sherry Lee, I am convinced that it is the most complete and tested systematic view of how the Pentecostal church should operate at this time in salvation history. This book distills a lifetime of practical experience, both in pastoring local churches and in classroom teaching. It is a great resource for pastors who need a new and exciting view of ministry in the twenty-first century.

—Vinson Synan
Dean Emeritus
Regent University, School of Divinity

I have a strong belief that a healthy church in every community is the only hope for America. The question is how do we get healthy? As superintendent of the North Texas District of the Assemblies, I prayerfully researched and searched for a process to move our pastors and churches on a path to health and effectiveness. My search ended when I discovered Church Life. We have now been in the process for just over two years; the results are very good and way beyond what I expected at this point in the process.

I do not mean to imply that it is a quick fix. It takes work and consistency, but if you are ready to see your church live up to its potential, you are ready for Church Life.

—Rick DuBose
Superintendent
North Texas District Assemblies of God

I had the privilege of learning the Church Life Model from Wayne and Sherry Lee. The principles they teach are easily applicable to any style of ministry. They also address the unique characteristics of a Spirit-filled church. Following their model will help any church grow broader and deeper.

—Rick Cole

Senior Pastor, Capital Christian Center,
Sacramento, CA

# THE CHURCH LIFE MODEL

## A Biblical Pattern for the Spirit-filled Church

Wayne and Sherry Lee

CREATION HOUSE

The Church Life Model: A Biblical Pattern for the Spirit-filled Church
by Wayne and Sherry Lee
Published by Creation House
A Charisma Media Company
600 Rinehart Road
Lake Mary, Florida 32746
www.charismamedia.com



Design Director: Bill Johnson
Cover design by Terry Clifton



Visit the author's Web site: www.churchliferesources.org.

Library of Congress Cataloging-in-Publication Data: 2011928571
International Standard Book Number: 978-1-61638-602-3

14 15 16 17 18 — 9 8 7 6 5 4 3
Printed in Canada

# ACKNOWLEDGMENTS

THE SUPPORT AND encouragement we received while working on this project strengthened us greatly. We could never list all the persons who deserve acknowledgment, but some of these persons helped us to make this book a reality. We acknowledge their commitment and assistance with deep gratitude.

- Friends and family for your support in words and prayers.
- Church Life consultants and coaches for participation with us in the work of the Kingdom.
- Church Life personnel, former and present. Special thanks to Timothy Hill, Jeremy Caffman, and David Lee.
- Those faithful friends who read the first manuscripts and gave us your thoughts: Joan Thomson, Pastor Greg Hackett, Pastor Ron Crum, and Robert and Diane Herron.
- Amanda Quain for your editorial expertise and guidance.
- Allen Quain and the publishing team at Creation House and Charisma Media.
- Jeremy Caffman for creation of the excellent graphics.
- David Lee for your media expertise during this project.
- The Church Life Survey participants.

# CONTENTS

## LIST OF DIAGRAMS

# PREFACE

*You yourselves are our letter, written on our hearts, known and read by everybody. You show that you are a letter from Christ, the result of our ministry, written not with ink but with the Spirit of the living God, not on tablets of stone but on tablets of human hearts.*

—2 Corinthians 3:2–3

WHAT A PRIVILEGE to live in the narrative of His story, the story of God and His people. What a joy to participate in His vision for all mankind and His mission for our generation. We gladly join Him in the work of His ministry on Earth, which spans from the Garden of Eden to the grand consummation of all things. The part He has directed us to do in this generation involves serving the church, His agent for kingdom mission in this world.

The words contained in this book are intended for the encouragement and edification of His church and His people. We desire to strengthen pastors and leaders so they, in turn, will strengthen and build up the body of Christ. We seek to bring clarity to some truths about the church. We offer these concepts for your discernment and judgment.

We acknowledge the influence of godly parents who gave us a spiritual legacy of faith that continues to sustain us. We cherish our children, who have joined us in Christ's ministry. We value our pastoral friends who have traveled with us as fellow sojourners, together with

Christ. We appreciate staff persons of our churches and Church Life Resources who have served with us. We prize our friends who have loved us through all of our stages of joy and struggle. We say thank you to all of those leaders who took a chance and partnered with us to offer the Church Life Model and principles to their constituents.

To acknowledge all those persons who have contributed to the concepts contained here would be impossible. Every moment we have been with Jesus, every hour we have served Him, every person we have met, every book we have read, every teacher we have received from, every idea we have entertained, every conversation we have had, every student who has participated in our classrooms, every support person who has helped us—all of these have contributed to the concepts we write in this book.

All love, honor, and glory belong to our Father.

—WAYNE H. LEE, DMIN
—SHERRY B. LEE, DMIN
LAKELAND, FLORIDA
FEBRUARY, 2011

# 1

# WHY WRITE ABOUT THE CHURCH LIFE MODEL?

*Now it is required that those who have been given* a trust must prove faithful.
—1 Corinthians 4:2, emphasis added

All authors have reasons for writing their books. Given the option of personal choice, we probably would never have found a reason to write one. Allow us to confess at the beginning that we write this book to prove faithful to a trust. We understand that many will read this book and question or perhaps even criticize that perspective. This can only prove valuable for both the authors and the readers, because books about the church, the body of Christ, should be read with discernment and judgment.

For the past fifteen to twenty years, our friends and peers have strongly urged us to write the principles of Church Life. They believe that persons who can never attend our pastoral groups and other training opportunities can benefit from these understandings about the church. Somehow, we never felt that the time had arrived to place our thoughts in print, and we never felt quite ready or capable to do so. Besides, both of us prefer communicating and interacting with pastors and leaders in face-to-face combat; giving a one-sided monologue of ideas and concepts with no opportunity for feedback, reflection, and clarification proves really difficult.

We have spent our lives loving, serving, and learning about the church. After our love for Christ, one another, and family, our affections focus upon His body and its leaders. We never tire of discovering new aspects about the church or coming together with others to dialogue about the church. To edify and build up the leaders and members of the church of Jesus Christ serves as a primary goal of our lives.

For the past six years, we have conducted numerous cohorts throughout the United States, and we have met many church leaders. God has given us the opportunity to speak to them about the church. Many persons have asked us to write these concepts and principles so they can share them with their church leaders and peers. For the past four years, we have pulled very close to some faithful pastors and leaders, seasoned men and women of faith, and we have reasoned and counseled together about the church. They have asked us to write our thoughts about the church so these understandings can benefit other leaders. For all of these reasons, we write this book.

When we first began this journey of discovery concerning the church, our goal involved helping pastors "get their arms around" the multifaceted work of leading and shepherding the people of God. We still have that goal. If any of the concepts shared here can make even one pastor's load lighter and his pathway clearer, we will have accomplished one of the key missions of our lives.

Finally, we write this book to complete the task given us by the Master. He has accompanied us on every trip. He has partnered with us in every cohort meeting. He has entrusted us with ideas and concepts we could never have perceived. So, we commit to prove faithful to His trust. We do the hard work of writing it here for you, the readers.

Writing about the church is a serious enterprise. We approach the task with great caution. We ask that readers receive only those thoughts and ideas that seem acceptable to them and to the Holy Spirit. Allow the Lord to emphasize the principles that He wants to accentuate in your place of ministry service.

## The Organization

The following chapters of this book provide an organized, progressive explanation of the development of the Church Life Model. In addition, the text offers ideas for utilization of the model in the local church. Feedback through survey results and comments from pastors who have engaged the model add significantly to the discussion.

The narrative of the book generally represents the combined voice of both authors. However, when the text uses the pronoun *I*, readers will know that Wayne speaks in that particular section.

Chapter 2 begins with the account of how the model developed from inception to stability. This chapter explains the beginnings and the formation of the model and also discusses the reasons the model has experienced receptivity among church leaders. This receptivity has greatly influenced the proliferation of the principles of Church Life.

Chapter 3 addresses the value of the model for local churches. Ten intrinsic values are identified and discussed in depth. The values derived from the model contribute greatly to its usefulness for the local church and its credibility among pastors and leaders.

Chapter 4 defines all of the functions (systems), quadrants, and the core of the schema. With a methodical movement around the model, each part and component is given consideration and discussion. When readers complete chapter 4, they will have a good working knowledge of the model as a simple church model. They will also understand how the model promotes health and vitality within the local church.

After an explanation of the components of the Church Life Model, the reader will now learn patterns to engage the model. Chapter 5 suggests ways that pastors, church leaders, and laity may engage the model in their local churches. Here, discussion about the Church Life Function Assessment also occurs. This chapter instructs readers in how to utilize this evaluative tool to assess the strengths and weaknesses of the systems of any church.

Chapter 6 gives the composite results of a Church Life Model survey conducted in February 2011. In this survey, pastors who have engaged the model responded to survey questions about the results of this engagement. These composite results provide good, non-scientific data based on their conclusions.

In the final chapter we will share plans for other publications. Also, directions are given for accessing additional resources and training from Church Life. A sample version of the Church Life Function Assessment appears in Appendix A. This short, 45-item, self-scored assessment will provide readers with an example of the statements that appear in the comprehensive 150-item Church Life Function Assessment. A sample prayer model can be found in Appendix B.

# 2

# WHAT IS THE CHURCH LIFE MODEL?

*Make this tabernacle and all its furnishings exactly like the pattern I will show you.*

—Exodus 25:9

## The Beginning

The Church Life Model offers church leaders a fresh perspective on the commonly known functions of the local church. Most people find very few of the concepts in this model as new information; however, they find the strategic placement and integration of these concepts within the schema captivating. The Church Life Model, derived from New Testament scriptural descriptions, presents a paradigm that identifies both the global and specific components of the church.

The dominant global conceptualizations of the church in the writings of Paul in the New Testament refer to this living, spiritual organism as the body with Christ as the functioning Head. Ephesians

1:22–23 states this straightforward theology: "And God placed all things under his feet and appointed him to be head over everything for the church, which is his body, the fullness of him who fills everything in every way." Ephesians 5:23 and Colossians 1:18 and 2:19 echo this perspective. First Corinthians 12 builds upon this concept to give further revelation about how the body functions under the headship of Christ.

In the Book of Acts, the apostle Luke describes the specific components of the ministry activity of the New Testament churches as they responded to the coming of the Holy Spirit upon them. Specifically, Acts 2:42–47 gives these terms: *teaching, fellowship, prayer, awe, wonders and signs, together, having in common, giving to needs, breaking bread, praising God, enjoying favor, adding numbers*, and *being saved*. These clearly stated functions of those who participated in the birthing of the church furnish the basics for the foundational systems of the Church Life Model.

The New Testament churches exuded vitality and health as they thrived, grew, reproduced, and expanded. They fulfilled Christ's mission to reach the known world with the gospel. They devoted themselves to God and to one another. They grew in Him as they exercised the gifts He gave them. They ministered within their contexts, revealing Christ's mercy and forgiveness to others.

Defining what this healthy, vital church should look like in contemporary terms and how it should function proved quite difficult for me. When I (Wayne) graduated from Asbury Theological Seminary with a Master of Divinity in 1972, I believed that I was prepared to pastor a local church. I knew well the hermeneutical process. My ability to understand the biblical languages was somewhat adequate. I had a great grasp of systematic theology. However, with all this in place, "I did not know what I did not know,"

"I did not know what I did not know," and I soon discovered that I did not know much about practical church ministry!

and I soon discovered that I did not know much about practical church ministry!

I entered my first job teaching pastoral ministry students in a Christian college. I quickly realized that training students for competent ministry involved much more than simply rehearsing my seminary notes. These notes, peppered with a few of my own uninformed notions, would not suffice for the substantial nuts-and-bolts equipment these eager learners needed to become adequate practitioners in the local church. During an appointment with the president of the college, I confessed my perceived inadequacy and asked his permission for a leave of two to three years to do the necessary research on the functions involved in ministry within the local church context. I asked if I could reapply for a position at the end of this venture. He agreed, and Sherry and I began the journey to get our minds and hearts around healthy church life. We did not realize that this journey would consume all of our lives.

Church life seemed rather simple from the viewpoint of a novice. The pastor preaches a little, prays a little, conducts worship services, visits the sick, does a bit of outreach, and supports missions. How difficult can that be? Now, after forty years of researching in the laboratory of the church, taking copious notes, and wrestling with the concepts, we have settled upon a model—the Church Life Model, defined and described in this book.

The model does not come from a theoretical perspective, although it reflects consideration and appropriate integration of the most current and reliable principles of church leadership and practice. The model integrates insights and learning from more than thirty years of practicing ministry in the local context of the Spirit-filled church and from more than ten years of teaching, refining, and testing the model as a professor, coach, and consultant.

Many moments of formation occurred along the journey with the development of the Church Life Model. A major piece of the process came in the early years of the 1980's when we began coaching and facilitating pastors in a cohort-style[1] gathering. Pastors and wives, most of them our friends in the ministry, convened for two to three days to engage in peer resourcing, better known to all of us at the time as our "pastoral survival cohort." Together the group struggled with the complexity of functions, drain of emotions, and waves of tasks demanded from us as current leaders and practitioners in the local church. We searched the biblical texts, mining ideas and concepts from the New Testament.

As we mentally and emotionally engaged in honest dialogue, the framework Sherry and I were working on shifted and turned repeatedly. Many times the complexity of the model would engulf us, and we would surface to gain clarity; other times the simplicity of the model motivated us to dig deeper, and we would penetrate new depths of understanding. Many hours of peer sharing and reflection within these groups added significantly to the formation and refinement of the healthy church model of church life that we now offer the church.

Many times the complexity of the model would engulf us, and we would surface to gain clarity; other times the simplicity of the model motivated us to dig deeper, and we would penetrate new depths of understanding.

## THE FORMATION

When seeking a comprehensive model of church life, first one looks to identify the multiple necessary components involved in the process of church life and pastoral ministry. In those first lists we made, over two hundred tasks emerged.

Working with such an unwieldy number presented great challenges for discussion and training in the early church life cohorts. Our goal for the training was to help pastors get their arms around church ministry so they could experience new levels of self-efficacy and confidence. However, the opposite often occurred. Church leaders left those early cohort sessions asking, "How can pastors possibly do all that the church demands?" Each session sent us back to the laboratory for more in-depth consideration and many hours of sorting concepts.

### The Fifteen Vital Functions

Long hours of studying the Scriptures, praying for discernment, listening to pastors, and burrowing into the entrails of the functioning of the church eventually advanced the formation of the Church Life Model to the next level. The next phase began with seeking to group the varied lists into larger constructs of meaning and activity. The components shifted, moved, and morphed for another five to seven years as the larger list of tasks began grouping into functions. At one point in the formation, the functions numbered as many as twenty-five; at another point, they numbered as few as thirteen.

All the while, training and sharing of the functions in cohort settings continued with passion and hunger. Even those early attempts to get one's arms around the process of healthy church life proved extremely clarifying and enlightening. Every session resulted in discernment from participants as they joined in thinking and praying for the church. None of the energy or time dissipated into thin air. All ideas and insights fell on listening ears—*our* listening ears that desired to find suitable and excellent avenues to understand and communicate with others the truths of church life.

All ideas and insights fell on listening ears—***our*** listening ears that desired to find suitable and excellent avenues to understand and communicate with others the truths of church life.

During this formation level, several writers influenced the establishment of the vital functions of church life. The most profound influence came from Kennon L. Callahan. In his book *Twelve Keys to an Effective Church*, Callahan writes, "Over these years of research and consultation, twelve factors have emerged persistently as the central characteristics of successful missional churches. These twelve fall into two categories: six are relational characteristics and six are functional characteristics."[2] The twelve factors offered by Callahan signaled that observing components of the church in order to increase effectiveness in church leadership could prove extremely beneficial. Callahan offered the following twelve keys:

> (1) specific, concrete missional objectives; (2) pastoral and lay visitation; (3) corporate, dynamic worship; (4) significant relational groups; (5) strong leadership resources; (6) streamlined structure and solid, participatory decision-making; (7) several competent programs and activities; (8) open accessibility; (9) high visibility; (10) adequate parking, land, and landscaping; (11) adequate space and facilities; (12) solid financial resources.[3]

Callahan's emphasis on observation, assessment, and strategic planning fired fresh ideas that impacted greatly our quest for a comprehensive list of components of healthy church life for Spirit-filled, Pentecostal, and Charismatic congregations. The investigation, research, and dialogue eventually served to solidify a list of fifteen vital functions. These fifteen functions or systems, like the organic systems of the human body, must operate with minimum stability if the body expects to live. They must operate with effectiveness and efficiency if the body expects to thrive. At this point, functions and systems became interchangeable words for church life. The fifteen vital functions of Church Life that formed in the early 1990's and remain today as hallmark systems of the Church Life Model are listed in Diagram 2A. These systems may have appeared in training sessions and training notebooks in varying orders and numbering; however, they were always presented as a list of the vital functions of church life.

These fifteen functions or systems, like the organic systems of the human body, must operate with minimum stability if the body expects to live.

**Fifteen Vital Functions**

1. Leadership
2. Vision/Mission
3. Spiritual Life
4. Preaching/Teaching
5. Worship
6. Assimilation
7. Care/Fellowship
8. Small Groups
9. Ministries
10. Discipleship
11. Evangelism/Missions
12. Public Relations
13. Decision-Making
14. Finances
15. Facilities

## Diagram 2A

### The Pastoral Roles or Quadrants

Now that the larger list of tasks had streamed into a list of the fifteen vital functions of church life, the next stage of model formation involved grouping the systems together in meaningful, strategic ways. While still working on the list of functions in the late 1980's and early 1990's, we traveled to the West Coast of the United States to participate in several conferences. Rising leaders in the church growth movement were speakers for these seminars and events, leaders such as Rick Warren, Bill Hybels, Carl George, Jack Hayford, Dale Galloway, Lyle Schaller, and Gordon MacDonald. These leaders shared many of their budding concepts in these seminars and later published books containing much of the same content. They not only shared what worked for them, but they also discussed some of the overall purposes and basic structural components of their approaches for the church, specifically the ones they were leading. The input of these persons at this phase assisted in the process of clustering the fifteen functions into larger concepts.

The first clustering of the systems simply came by asking, "Do any of these systems fit together?" Somewhere along the path of this inquiry, the thought occurred that the systems might fit into larger pastoral roles. A role, like the role of husband, carries multiple responsibilities and meaning. Roles are large concepts that contain many constructs. Testing the idea of roles with existing church life cohort groups and other leaders helped us to get comfortable using these constructions. After testing the idea with several persons and groups, the following role groupings emerged. (See Diagram 2B.)

| **Pastoral Roles** | **Functions** |
|---|---|
| **Visionary Leadership** | 1. Leadership<br>2. Vision/Mission |
| **Spiritual Life** | 3. Spiritual Life<br>4. Preaching/Teaching<br>5. Worship |
| **Spiritual Community** | 6. Assimilation<br>7. Care/Fellowship<br>8. Small Groups |
| **Ministries** | 9. Ministries<br>10. Discipleship |
| **Outreach** | 11. Evangelism/Missions<br>12. Public Relations |
| **Management** | 13. Decision-Making<br>14. Finances<br>15. Facilities |

**DIAGRAM 2B**

Clustering the functions or systems within major roles made sense to those persons engaging in our cohorts. Leadership and vision/mission joined to describe the *visionary leadership* role. The systems of spiritual life, preaching/teaching, and worship fit well into the role of *spiritual life director*. The role of *spiritual community facilitator* provided a home for the functions of assimilation, care/fellowship, and small groups. Ministries and discipleship were placed well within the role of *ministries director*, just as evangelism/missions and public relations found acceptance in the role of *outreach director*. The mirror role of *visionary leadership* is the *management* role. The *management* role incorporated easily the functions of decision-making, finances, and facilities.

Showing this placement of the fifteen functions clustered into six basic roles propelled the Church Life paradigm into a new stage of understanding for persons engaging the model in their local contexts. The receptivity was overwhelming. Now leaders could envision themselves in multiple roles of leadership aligning with missional activities revealed in the New Testament churches. Pastors involved in church life cohorts during this stage communicated that the job of pastoring felt more manageable and also became more manageable for them.

Likewise, communication between pastors and their church leaders reached new levels. Defining the roles and grouping the functions within the church environment gave more pronounced definition to the missional activity within the church. Members and leaders could more readily identify opportunities for ministry engagement.

Defining the roles and grouping the functions within the church environment gave more pronounced definition to the missional activity within the church.

This stage of formation probably stands as the most significant for the Church Life Model. The alignment of systems within pastoral roles, which soon became recognized as the missional roles of the church, brought great clarity. At the same time, this movement also ushered in the last stage of formation for the model, the assignment of a compelling diagram.

**The Church Life Model Diagram**

Formation of the Church Life Model to this stage involved identifying the multiple tasks of the church, streaming these tasks through identified systems, and then clustering those systems (or functions) into specific roles. This formation process required years of untold hours in focused study, observation, and testing. When we first began the process, we never intended to propose a model of church life. The time spent investigating scriptures, practicing ministry, and dialoguing with colleagues focused upon one goal—identifying the vital components of the local church so leaders could understand the full scope of the work of church ministry and learn to minister well to bring health and vitality to the local church in its unique context. However, a model did emerge.

Over a five-year period, as the need developed to communicate clearly the components—the roles (quadrants) and functions—of the Church Life Model, the parts began forming into a compelling diagram. Some have jokingly referred to the diagram as "the circle of life"; others call it the Church Life Wheel, while yet others describe it as the Church Life Pie. Diagram 2C graphically illustrates the model.

## Diagram 2C

Diagram 2C illustrates the Church Life Model that has solidified since 2004. Variations of the model can be found dating before this year, but the model has remained static since early 2004. A few minor revisions in the graphic have occurred, but the overall paradigm has stabilized.

The inner circle serves as the core. The core, often called the *leadership core*, comprises the leadership and management roles, two sides of one coin. Leadership provides energy toward the future of the church; management organizes the chaos to accomplish the vision of the church. Leadership and management must occur in each of the quadrant ministry roles. So, these two vital roles are situated inside the central core of the church so they can touch each ministry quadrant.

The four ministry roles are known as the quadrants, or the missional roles, of the church. Each quadrant, one through four, serves as a missional focus. The church connects people to God in the *spiritual life quadrant* and then to one another in the *spiritual community quadrant.* People of the church participate in spiritual formation in quadrant three, *the ministries quadrant,* while also finding their specific areas of spiritual giftedness and service to those inside and outside the church. People connect with the external community through evangelism and missions in quadrant four, *the outreach quadrant,* and also help to build the church's good name through excellent public relations.

The power of this biblical model lies in its strategic placement and integration of known concepts into an understandable schema.

The Church Life Model effectively depicts the components of the church. It captivates the attention of church leaders, and it enjoys great receptivity among experienced pastors. It assists them in mentally organizing the plethora of tasks, activities, responsibilities, and components that inevitably catch them in a whirlpool of endless motion. As noted at the beginning of this chapter, the Church Life Model presents a fresh perspective on the commonly known functions of the local church. The concepts in the model contain little new information. The power of this biblical model lies in its strategic placement and integration of known concepts into an understandable schema.

## The Receptivity

In late 2004, after over twenty years of prayerful research, development, and testing, Church Life Resources launched multiple Church Life cohorts within the United States. In these groups, the Church Life

Model and its components comprised the centerpiece of training. The model served as the baseline for the healthy church. In addition, pastors attending these groups assessed their local churches using the 150-item Church Life Function Assessment. With this assessment they could evaluate the strengths and weaknesses of the fifteen vital functions as they existed in their congregations.

Approaching the dialogue of church health with a model and a comprehensive assessment of each component of that model has met with overwhelming receptivity. Not only do church leaders in these cohort environs grapple with the health of their churches using the Church Life Model as a baseline, but they also strategize for advancement utilizing a "change model." (This change, or transformation, model will be the subject of a later publication.)

The Church Life Model has been met with great receptivity for several reasons. First, the model resonates with experienced practitioners because they now can visualize familiar as well as unfamiliar components of the church in a strategic pattern that makes sense. Although no one intends this result, some have contended that training for pastoral leadership of the church proved scattered, piecemeal, and downright confusing for them. An open, comprehensive paradigm based upon biblical principles and user-friendly structures that fit any context provides a workable framework for pastors to view and implement church activity.

Having a Christian worldview is important for relating correctly with the world, but having a Christ-centered, biblical view of the church is mandatory for relating correctly with the church.

Second, the model emanates from the scriptural descriptors of the New Testament church. It gives precedence to the facts that the church is a living organism with Jesus as the Head (Eph. 1:22) and that without Him "you can do nothing" (John 15:5). Having a Christian worldview is important for relating correctly with the world, but having a Christ-centered, biblical view of the church is mandatory for relating correctly with the church. Confusing these two relational spheres produces much dissonance in the practice of ministry.

Third, the model recognizes that the church exists as the body of Christ and yet has innate organization within and among its systems, just as the human body organizes around human functional systems (1 Cor. 12). The church lives as an organism because of the living Christ, who functions as Head, and because of the Spirit, who gives life. Yet it also qualifies as an organization that integrates systems, functions, activities, and ministries for mission accomplishment. This dual orientation reminds us that the church of Jesus Christ reflects both incarnational, spiritual being as well as physical being.

Fourth, the model closely adheres to the missional goals of the kingdom, spoken by the Master. Obedience to the central mandates of Christ found in the Great Commandment and the Great Commission occupies the central focus of the framework. These mandates and how they comprise the missional focus of the model will be discussed in depth in chapter 3.

This dual orientation reminds us that the church of Jesus Christ reflects both incarnational, spiritual being as well as physical being.

Fifth, the model does assist leaders in getting their arms around the work of ministry in the local church. Grouping multiple tasks into systems and integrating these into meaningful roles of ministry build health and vitality into the structures of the local church. The Church Life Model benefits pastors in understanding how the systems of the church work together to align church activities toward vision and mission accomplishment. Competent church pastors who can see the comprehensive nature of the work of the church can lead local churches into health and vitality.

The following comments were provided by pastors and other leaders who have utilized the Church Life Model in their ministry contexts. These comments, and many others not written here, assure us that the Church Life Model offers a viable paradigm of church health and vitality for today's local church. The enthusiastic receptivity of practitioners, who have tested the model in many settings, attests to the validity of this healthy church model.

> The Church Life Model is the most comprehensive organizational understanding of internal and external church leadership and ministry design I have discovered. I was struggling with understanding the big picture connection of ministries and leadership when Church Life, ten years ago, provided the model and map for our future at King's River. Developmental growth promoting healthy, balanced life with inexhaustible structures and expansions of vision and mission are possible through Church Life.
>
> —Pastor Ron Crum
> King's River Worship Center
> Charleston, West Virginia

> Our association's journey with Church Life has produced both an increase in total numbers of resourced leaders and a higher level of health within our churches. Additionally, our region continues to grow healthy leaders who grow healthy ministries. Church Life helps the pastors and leaders process key growth issues and identify barriers associated with plateau or decline. Our region is no longer crystallized, and new growth continues to emerge—both in leadership development and ministry models of health.
>
> —Pastor Jim Beaird
> Regional Executive Director, Southeast Region
> of Open Bible Churches
> Valrico, Florida

> The Church Life Model serves as a holistic picture of the church, identifying the fifteen vital functions that are essential to a healthy and vibrant church. It aids in understanding the indispensable biblical components that are crucial to the life of the church and how they relate to one another. It is fully Pentecostal in that it realizes the necessity of the Spirit to breathe life upon every aspect of the church and to guide and

direct in the fulfillment of mission. This is our third time through the two-year process, and it has been very beneficial in bringing a greater cohesiveness in our church body. The process enables more people to embrace the vision and become engaged in its fulfillment. A visiting evangelist commented that he sensed something different in our congregation. He described it as "harnessed passion."

—PASTOR MARIA KHALEEL
NEW LIFE ASSEMBLY OF GOD
PEMBROKE PINES, FLORIDA

Church Life gives a paradigm that provides a practical Pentecostal ecclesiology for the pastor to build a Spirit-filled church. The process promotes the development of a custom, strategic plan in accordance with the church's individual DNA. The process is not built on a model that will change but on a systematic concept that will endure time.

—PASTOR JIMMY WHITE, DMIN
NORTHSIDE ASSEMBLY OF GOD
TEXARKANA, TEXAS

It doesn't take long to realize that ministry is an overwhelming privilege. Initially it appears to be a floating cloud of random parts filled with all the good things we should be doing. Finding a way to bring peace to those parts and embrace all that Christ's body is supposed to be seems impossible. Most ministry models address these issues skin deep or are so tight that they do not allow the natural flow of the Spirit. Church Life is a strategic, comprehensive approach to ministry that leaves all the windows open so the Spirit can breathe life into the local church. I have adopted the Church Life approach to ministry because I simply have not found anything better.

—PASTOR JAY WEST
KINGWOOD CHURCH
BIRMINGHAM, ALABAMA

*How do we grow the North Texas District from 540 churches to 1,000 healthy churches?* was the daunting question and subsequent task I was given upon accepting a leadership role in Target 1000. In order to accomplish this monumental goal, we first needed a Pentecostal *process* to connect both our traditional and contemporary congregations. In the same vein, we needed a replicable *system* that would lift any congregation to the next level. Finally, we needed a *model* that would help our pastors clearly identify how a healthy church functions. After an exhaustive examination of current church health models, Church Life's model was the only model that met our requirements and exceeded our expectations. Since implementing this model, our churches have strengthened in number and attained new levels of health.

—Mike Harper
North Texas District of the Assemblies of God
Director of Target 1000
Waxahachie, Texas

In February 2011, I pulled together a group of church leaders in the European context to test receptivity to the Church Life Model. These European International churches and congregations of all sizes found the Church Life Model language clear and its principles universal and comprehensive. The roles, functions, and constructs hit no walls of resistance or contextualization issues. The model was embraced by the participants as a tool that will help us reach new levels of effectiveness and impact. The largest problem I see in the future is meeting the demands for further resources from Church Life for European churches.

—Pastor Tom Manning
Assemblies of God Missionary
Senior Pastor, Vienna Christian Center

## THE WIND OF THE SPIRIT

Although we have attempted to share the story of the formation of the Church Life Model, we could not leave out the most defining piece. Throughout the process of observation and discernment, the wind of the Holy Spirit determined the direction and ordered the steps. Even while attempting to write the story of the formation of the Church Life Model, difficulty arises when asking questions like, When did this come together? and, What steps of development occurred in this stage?

The awesome fact remains that the model would not exist and would not have found fertile soil in multiple settings today were it not for the powerful work of the Holy Spirit. Prayer occurred at each stage of the journey. The first formation stages were insight and faith-walks with the Spirit of discernment. How does one know? One knows when truth appears. Those precious moments of insight will remain with us forever. To say that we experienced His anointing for the formulation stages of the Church Life Model would be such a grave understatement.

How does one know? One knows when truth appears. Those precious moments of insight will remain with us forever.

In succeeding stages, the wind blew forcefully upon our backs, strengthening us and propelling us along in the journey. The launch stages felt like the strong breath of the Spirit blowing upon His church. It came as a lifting wind of renewal and refreshment upon those who opened their hearts. The wind has touched many pastors and churches; many more remain ahead. Proliferation of the Church Life Model among the churches of America has occurred *only* by the wind of His Spirit.

# 3

# WHAT VALUE DOES THE MODEL OFFER LOCAL CHURCHES?

*Now it's up to you. Be on your toes—both for yourselves and your congregation of sheep. The Holy Spirit has put you in charge of these people—God's people they are—to guard and protect them. God himself thought they were worth dying for.*

—Acts 20:28, The Message

Answering the question "What is the Church Life Model?" in the previous chapter helped with understanding how the model began and developed. In this chapter, attention will focus on the question of the value of the model for local churches.

Many models of local church ministry exist. The value of any model for the local church setting rests upon its credibility and usefulness. This chapter explores the ten values of the Church Life Model for local ministry. These values are listed and defined in Diagram 3A.

| Value | Definition |
|---|---|
| **Missional** | Engages the church in the missional work of Christ |
| **Universal** | Fits any church, any place, any time, any size |
| **Comprehensive** | Includes all the components of the church |
| **Spirit-filled, Pentecostal** | Embraces a New Testament view of church ministry |
| **Developmental** | Promotes a process-oriented, sequential growth mode |
| **Systemic** | Embraces a systems approach to the church body |
| **Visual** | Owns a diagram of parts fitted into a meaningful whole |
| **Structural** | Promotes structural alignment in all functions |
| **Apostolic** | Allows constituents to function as the people of God |
| **Unifying** | Promotes unified nomenclature and semantics to enhance communication |

## DIAGRAM 3A

## A MISSIONAL MODEL

The Church Life Model is a missional model. When churches employ the model, they engage the church and its constituents in the missional work of Christ in His kingdom. God has a vision; He is on a mission. When the church joins Christ in the work He desires to do through the local church, then the congregation receives the benefit of missional health and strength.

What is the mission of Jesus? When queried by the religious scholars of His day concerning the greatest commandment of the Law, Jesus replied, "Love the Lord your God with all your heart and with all your soul and with all your mind. This is the first and greatest commandment. And the second is like it: 'Love your neighbor as yourself.' All the Law and the Prophets hang on these two commandments" (Matt. 22:37–40). These words provide clarity of mission. The first order of business for a person or a church is total involvement with God. And the second order is total involvement with the community of believers.

Quadrant one of the Church Life Model connects people to God in meaningful ways through the functions of spiritual life, preaching/teaching, and worship. Quadrant two connects people to one another in assimilation of new persons into the church, in care and fellowship among the members, and in small groups. So, the right half of the Church Life Model involves the constituents of the church in the *Great Commandment* of Christ.

Likewise, quadrants three and four advance constituents of the church into the *Great Commission*. Jesus commanded believers before He ascended to "go and make disciples of all nations, baptizing them in the name of the Father and of the Son and of the Holy Spirit, teaching them to obey everything I have commanded you" (Matt. 28:19–20). Quadrant three of the Church Life Model provokes spiritual growth and ministry growth, as well as awareness of spiritual giftedness. Quadrant four thrusts these growing Christians into "going" into their communities to evangelize, teach, and model. So, the left half of the Church Life Model, quadrants three and four, serves to move believers into the *Great Commission*.

> No other vision and mission exists, except that spoken to the church by the Head, Jesus Christ. His sole desire for the souls of all humankind moves in and through the functions of the missional quadrants.

Engaging church constituents in the missional quadrants of the Church Life Model integrates all ministries into this unified vision and mission of Christ. As a result, unhealthy ministries, such as silo ministries, which feed upon their own energy and exist only for the advantage of the participants, are exposed. Weighed down with personal, human agenda and unable to give to others, such ministries soon dissipate because of the unifying effect of integrating the systems and aligning the quadrants with the overall vision and mission of the church. Clear focus upon the visionary heart of the Father breeds health and generates life.

Not all expressions of the vision or mission will look the same. Each church will express the unique vision that God determined for that local body when He birthed it. Each body will have a different face, different and unique characteristics, and a different context to reach. Each church must, however, involve its members in the vision and mission of Christ in all of its tasks, in each of its functions or systems, and in each of the quadrants.

Love and worship God, love others, disciple, and go into the world—these missional hallmarks of the ministry of Jesus make up the missional quadrants of the Church Life Model. When leaders and churches engage in the model, they join the vision and mission of God for the world. No other vision and mission exists, except that spoken to the church by the Head, Jesus Christ. His sole desire for the souls of all humankind moves in and through the functions of the missional quadrants.

## A Universal Model

The Church Life Model is a universal model. It offers only principles and no programs. Principles transcend cultures, location, size, and generations. The model works in all settings because it rests firmly upon biblical principles. The fifteen functions or systems exist in every church on Planet Earth. Therefore, the model works for churches in China and Chicago, in urban and rural America, in mega churches of thousands, and in church plants of ten.

The Church Life Model has recently crossed the waters into the continents of the world. The feedback from churches from other nations of the world confirms the universal nature of the model. The model prospers among the churches of Latin America and in the churches of Africa and Europe.

Church planters attend Church Life cohorts and engage the model while working through the initial stages of birthing a church. Reports confirm that just as a newborn baby has complete human systems, so do infant churches. The model works as well for infant churches as it does for churches of thousands. The universal value of the Church Life Model will be confirmed as churches in all settings engage and utilize it.

Imbedding principles into a church rather than loading the church down with programs promotes health and vitality. Because leaders look for the latest and best programs, many churches are put together piecemeal. They exist as a patchwork of imported programs that work well in other locations with other people with different needs. Engaging the Church Life Model assists leaders in shedding programs that do not work, bringing alignment and integration within the systems and quadrants and restoring healthy functioning based upon biblical principles.

How can one lead an entity that appears nebulous or has moving, unnamed components? The Church Life Model seeks to name the parts—all of the parts.

## A Comprehensive Model

Most pastors who embrace the Church Life Model attest that its greatest value lies in its comprehensiveness. By *comprehensive*, they mean the model brings all the necessary components of church life together for consideration and evaluation. No large components are missing from the paradigm. Most existing church models do not seek to be comprehensive models; the Church Life Model does.

Comprehensiveness is a major factor in evaluation. Assessment of all major components of the church contributes significantly to a realistic understanding of all the strengths and weaknesses of the church. The converse is also true. When all of the pieces do not receive evaluation, a realistic assessment may not occur.

A major difficulty for pastors and church leaders arises from their inability to "get their arms around" the mammoth job of leading the church. How can one lead an entity that appears nebulous or has moving, unnamed components? The Church Life Model seeks to name the parts—all of the parts. Over time, many groups have received the challenge to find those major, or even minor, missing pieces. It is believed that every major component one desires to address concerning the church may be found in this comprehensive model.

## A Spirit-filled, Pentecostal Model

The Church Life Model is a Pentecostal model because it emanates from the descriptors provided by the New Testament. Our educational training in Christian colleges, universities, and seminaries alerted us that not all agree on what a Pentecostal paradigm of ministry involves. However, the Bible states clearly the prevalent activity of the Holy Spirit within the New Testament churches. So, whether one uses the term *Pentecostal*, *Charismatic*, *Spirit-filled*, or *Spirit-led* makes little difference for the purpose of this dialogue. Gordon Fee observes in his book *Paul, the Spirit, and the People of God*, "The Spirit must be reinstated into the Trinity, where he has never been excluded in our creeds and liturgies, but has been practically excluded from the experienced life of the church. To be a Pauline Christian means to take the Spirit with full seriousness as the way the eternal God is ever present with his people."[1] This declaration echoes the sentiments of Pentecostal believers, especially those of us who have enjoyed the privilege of a heritage that emphasizes the Spirit-filled life. The presence of God must invade meetings of the people of God; otherwise, they meet for their own purposes to fulfill human agenda. The Church Life Model is a Spirit-filled model because it accentuates

> The Church Life Model is a Spirit-filled model because it accentuates the necessity of the presence of God meeting with His people, as the Spirit met with the believers of the first century.

the necessity of the presence of God meeting with His people, as the Spirit met with the believers of the first century.

Second, the Church Life Model is a Pentecostal paradigm because of where it begins. The first function of quadrant one is spiritual life—devotional time with God, private prayer, and public prayer. Just as Acts opens with an Upper Room prayer meeting mandated by Christ to His followers before His ascension, the Church Life Model devotes the first movement of the first missional quadrant to prayer for the power to accomplish Christ's mission in the church.

> On one occasion, while he was eating with them, he gave them this command: "Do not leave Jerusalem, but wait for the gift my Father promised, which you have heard me speak about. For John baptized with water, but in a few days you will be baptized with the Holy Spirit."
>
> —Acts 1:4–5

These were some of the last words He gave us—wait for the Holy Spirit, the power to witness. Azusa Street in Los Angeles, California, the site of one of the hallmark movements of the Pentecostals, followed the same pattern. This humble house was a place of prayer from which God initiated a worldwide wave of mission. Pray first, seek Him first, discern His vision and mission first, receive His Spirit first—this is the biblical pattern. Nestle close to God, not culture, to discern and accomplish God's mission.

Pray first, seek Him first, discern His vision and mission first, receive His Spirit first—this is the biblical pattern. Nestle close to God, not culture, to discern and accomplish God's mission.

So, the Church Life Model encourages church leaders to sense and know the activity of God among them. At first, discerning this activity may prove a challenge, but as the senses become trained to hear the voice of God and spiritual eyes begin to search for the activity of Christ working by the power of the Spirit, then discovering what God desires to accomplish becomes clearer indeed. God has always had a mission; He works even now among His body. Can you see Him?

## A Developmental Model

Life is developmental; church life is developmental. Most patterns of the church appear hollow and flat, lacking movement and dynamic. Not so with the Church Life Model. The vital parts of the paradigm work together to promote a life-giving, sequential process of encounter with distinct expressions of the Spirit. Thus, growth and advancement occur in both leaders and churches.

This continual cycle of ever-escalating spiritual development generates unusual levels of spiritual life within the person and the church.

First, one encounters the renewing, restoring Spirit of God, the *pneuma*, and builds a strong relationship with Him. Second, one engages the spiritual community, the *koinonia,* and actualizes the truth that the church with all its members belongs to God and lives in His face, His sight. Third, one grows into Christlikeness by ministering to others and employing spiritual gifts in ministry settings. Fourth, one reproduces, expressing fruitfulness both through personal maturity and through adding others to the kingdom. This continual cycle of ever-escalating spiritual development generates unusual levels of spiritual life within the person and the church. A church grows developmentally the same as an individual—connect in new, fresh ways to God, connect relationally to others, mature in ministry and spiritual gifts, and reach others by connecting them to God. So, the developmental value of the Church Life Model contributes significantly to the overall spiritual dynamic of the church.

## A Systemic Model

Another value the Church Life Model offers the local church is a systems approach. Paul, in 1 Corinthians 12, provides the comparison of the body of Christ to the human body. Specifically, he compares members of the church to the eyes and the hands of the human body.

When one refers to the church as a system, this implies that each of the systems of the church impact all the other systems; thus, each affects the whole. In the Church Life paradigm, each of the fifteen vital functions provides either health or weakness, dependent upon the degree of vitality of the particular system.

The analogy holds true for the human body concerning human systems. If one experiences weakness in the digestive or respiratory systems, this lack of health contributes to the overall condition of the person. Conversely, when health returns to these systems, the whole body experiences the benefits and strengthens. So it is with the body of Christ. A church having weak spiritual life or weak care culture suffers in its overall health. However, when these systems renew and begin to function properly, health returns.

A systems approach implies, as well, that the system resists change in order to protect itself. In this way, systems in a church compare well to family systems. Norman Shawchuck and Roger Heuser, in *Managing the Congregation*, apply family systems theory to the religious organization. They discuss homeostasis, the tendency for systems to remain static and unchanged; they elaborate on both its benefits and challenges for the church system. "The same forces that shape the feeling of family togetherness in a congregation are the same forces that hinder change."[2]

Engaging a systems approach through the Church Life Model gives a church the opportunity to assign new roles, to reculture, and to restructure with intentionality.

Church systems hold together with strong cords of spoken and unspoken beliefs, behaviors, and roles just as family systems. Persons in a family acquire roles and prescribed behaviors over time; so do leaders in church systems. Engaging a systems approach through the Church Life Model gives a church the opportunity to assign new roles, to reculture, and to restructure with intentionality. Although longstanding structures of interaction and behavior provide security for a group, they must not promote dysfunction or prevent healthful movement and change. These understandings of systems assist leaders in moving their church family toward change, health, and vitality.

## A VISUAL MODEL

Scriptures support the idea of visual models. When God asked Moses to build a tabernacle for the wilderness journey, He instructed him carefully: "Make this tabernacle and all its furnishings exactly like the pattern I will show you" (Exod. 25:9). The visual scenes of water baptism and the Lord's Supper endure as visible patterns given so one can replicate the actions in obedience to His commands. As such a visual pattern, the Church Life Model assists pastors and leaders in seeing the parts of the biblical church and how the parts fit into and contribute to the whole.

As such a visual pattern, the Church Life Model assists pastors and leaders in seeing the parts of the biblical church and how the parts fit into and contribute to the whole.

What do you see when you view the church? What one sees will determine how one relates to and interacts with it. If one sees the church as a large gathering on Sunday mornings, then attendance on Sunday adequately meets the requirements of church involvement. If one sees the church as a place to receive teaching, then participating in a teaching opportunity meets the requirements of involvement. What one sees defines the church; what one sees is of great significance.

The visual model of the church helps leaders to view the church objectively. As pastors swirl in the demands of the multiple tasks, they often become engulfed and lose objectivity. As leaders, however, engage the Church Life Model, they develop the skill of stepping back from the fray of activity that usually exists in the church. As they step back, they can identify the parts and note how those significant parts fit together and intersect with one another. This objectivity helps pastors to de-personalize what occurs in the church; he or she begins to view matters from a different viewpoint.

A valuable and lasting visual paradigm has both simplicity and complexity. It provides windows of in-depth meaning as well as simple structures that one may quickly memorize. The Church Life schema is a visual model that invites such in-depth investigation. Each of the fifteen functions of church life could easily serve as the topic of a complete book or manual. At the same time, the schema stands as a simple model of the components that function within the church. Its visual simplicity makes the church visible to even the casual observer.

## A Structural Model

Churches are both organisms and organizations. Without structure the organism accomplishes little. The design has much influence upon the outcome or product of any organization. A great value of the Church Life Model rests in its structural design, which brings alignment toward vision and mission accomplishment. Effective configurations of the church organize and facilitate both the divine and human energy of the organism. Ministry within the organism flows along the structural boundaries created for mission accomplishment. These structures give permission, grant authority, and provide opportunity for ministry release. Church constructs either release or restrict the activity of Christ in His body.

Church constructs either release or restrict the activity of Christ in His body.

Many churches consist of twisted, complicated structures. Often programs, staff, and vision initiatives are disconnected and unaligned. The Church Life Model brings leaders, ministries, and programs into alignment with the overall mission and specific missional goals of the church so both the divine and human energy can have optimum impact.

The Bible neither supports nor promotes a particular organizational design. God uses many, and almost any, structures. However, all structures are not equal. Most churches simply allow configurations for ministry to evolve during certain developmental stages, eventually causing dysfunction. The dysfunction occurs because structures that accommodate growth at one stage may impede advancement at the next developmental stage. As this discussion advances, the flexible, simple, sequential, accommodating, comprehensive, and process-oriented nature and design of the Church Life Model will become evident.

Through the design of its missional quadrants and functional systems, the Church Life Model aligns the processes of all the ministries of the church with the vision and mission of Christ. A church with fifty to one hundred congregants can utilize the structure of the Church Life Model to assist them in organizing ministry in balance with their limited time and resources. At the same time, a church of eight hundred to one thousand can remain missionally focused while adding multiple, need-satisfying ministries. This framework provides a structural model that welcomes the presence and activity of Christ and then propels all of the spiritual energy of the organism toward fulfilling God's vision and mission of that particular people in that particular context.

## AN APOSTOLIC MODEL

An apostolic model of ministry motivates constituents to function as the people of God. The Church Life Model is an apostolic model. The paradigm promotes strongly the truth that the people of God comprise the body, and Christ is the functioning Head of that body. The members are the called people of God, with gifts and abilities given by the Spirit. Church Life advocates recognition of the callings and giftedness of each member within the spiritual community of the local church. Also, certain role-gifts have been given to leaders in the church. These role-gifts are listed in Ephesians 4:11—apostle, prophet, pastor, teacher, and evangelist.

The paradigm promotes strongly the truth that the people of God comprise the body, and Christ is the functioning Head of that body.

The Church Life Model, because it mirrors the New Testament

church, easily accommodates recognition of these role-gifts listed in Ephesians. The following graphic (Diagram 3B) helps one to know where each role-gift given to the church by Christ fits within the missional quadrants.

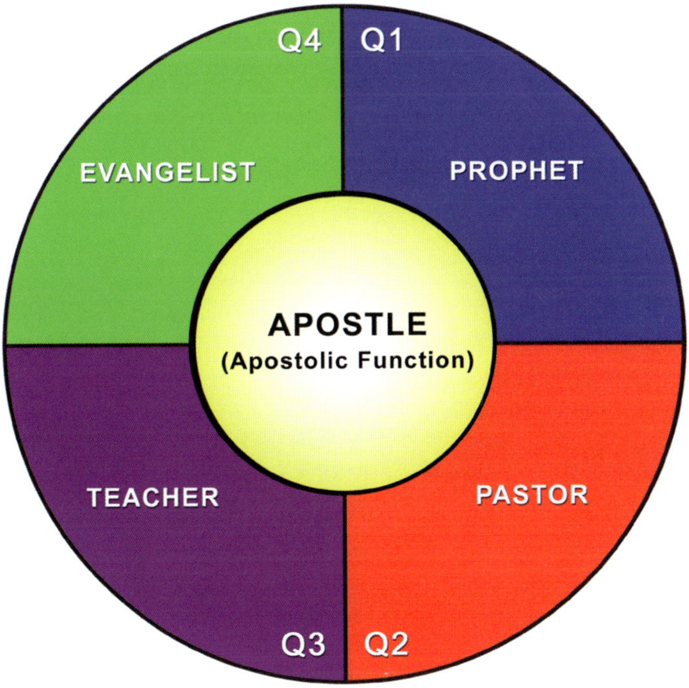


### Diagram 3B

Identifying the personal role-gifts of church leaders assists them in discovering where they might best fit into ministries within the church. Persons having strong pastoral gifts should seek ministry opportunities in the spiritual community quadrant (Q2) while those with the gift of evangelism should seek out ministries in the outreach quadrant (Q4). The same would be true for those having the role-gifts of prophet—the spiritual life quadrant (Q1)—or teacher, the ministries quadrant (Q3).

The role of the apostolic function, however, often causes misgivings for those who take issue with identifying any leaders as apostles. We certainly believe that caution is warranted in this matter. However, the apostolic role signals strong giftings in both leadership and management. Leaders who manifest the apostolic function in the areas of missionary work and church planting seem reasonable to most and enjoy more acceptance. We would contend, however, that the apostolic function was given to the church just as the role-gifts of pastor, teacher, or evangelist were given. Corporate business literature uses the word *entrepreneurship* to define the leader/manager of the corporate world. Some of the physical work of the apostolic function parallels this type of leader.

A healthy church cannot occur without the proper working of the leaders' gifts within the body.

In the Church Life Model, all five roles are acknowledged and encouraged for the growth and health of the body. As Ephesians 4:12-13 asserts, these gifts are given to prepare God's people "for works of service, so that the body of Christ may be built up ... and become mature, attaining to the whole measure of the fullness of Christ." A healthy church cannot occur without the proper working of the leaders' gifts within the body.

## A Unifying Model

Last, but perhaps the most important value of the Church Life Model, is the unity it brings to those pastors, churches, districts, or regions that engage in dialogue about the church utilizing its framework. The model clearly promotes a unified nomenclature and semantic that enhances this communication. With this schema, everyone can get on the same page. The arrangement of functions into quadrants and the core makes it easy to talk about the church in respectful, Christ-honoring ways. When dialogue ensues about the systems or functions, everyone can enter the dialogue and contribute because of familiarity with the topics. So, in reality, the paradigm brings great clarity and focus to the discussion of the church.

The model also brings unity to leaders within the local church.

Leaders in certain areas of missional thrust within the church often suffer from "mission myopia." They convince themselves—and those who serve with them—that the function of ministry they provide is the most important to God and the church. In fact, some even suggest that this one function may be the total sum of all the church must accomplish. When the church engages the Church Life Model, leaders began to respect and become more aware of the multi-functional nature of the church. We are not saying that the schema will cure mission myopia, but we do say the model unifies church leaders and aligns them to accomplish the multifaceted vision God intends for His church.

When the church engages the Church Life Model, leaders began to respect and become more aware of the multi-functional nature of the church.

In chapter 1 the question "What is the Church Life Model?" served as the focus of discussion. In this chapter, the conversation moved forward to consideration of the value of utilizing the Church Life Model in the local church. Ten essential values were offered and discussed to provide reasonable assurance of the model's credibility and usefulness. Now this discourse will progress into the fifteen vital systems or functions that fill this paradigm and, at the same time, bring life and health to the church.

# 4

# WHAT ARE THE FIFTEEN VITAL FUNCTIONS OF THE CHURCH LIFE MODEL?

*Each of us finds our meaning and function as a part of his body*

—Romans 12:5, The Message

CHAPTER 1 GAVE the historical development and an explanation of the components of the Church Life Model. Hopefully by this point you have developed some familiarity with the model, its parts, and its organization. A brief discussion of each of the fifteen vital functions will occur in this chapter. Also, consideration will be given to how the functions integrate and intersect within each quadrant.

Before a surgeon can operate on a patient, she needs a comprehensive knowledge of the human body and specialized understanding of the part of the body needing surgery. The same holds true for the church. Pastors need both a comprehensive and specialized knowledge of the components of the body of Christ before attempting operations. This vital functions approach takes time; the training is long-term. The approach attempts to make visible the invisible ministry reality that exists in the church. Observations of this approach are accurate only to the extent that they describe spiritual reality. So, view this attempt to make these invisible realities concrete as a human project flawed by limited understanding but having powerful potential under the guidance of the Holy Spirit.

The central core of the Church Life Model contains two divisions—the top of the core (C1) and the bottom of the core (C2). Situated in the top of the core is the larger role of leadership, while the management role occupies the bottom of the core. These dual roles of leadership and management must intersect with each of the quadrants, so they lay strategically in the center of the model. They reflect two sides of one coin: leaders lead, then they manage. Effectiveness determines the health of the leadership role, and efficiency determines the health of management. Both have equal impact upon the health of the church; however, the time and energy devoted to each of these roles are not equal. Leading demands 35 to 40 percent of the pastor's time, while managing requires 60 to 65 percent. Each of the ministry quadrants needs both leadership and management time from the leaders of the church.

They reflect two sides of one coin: leaders lead, then they manage. Effectiveness determines the health of the leadership role, and efficiency determines the health of management.

The numbering (one through fifteen) and listing of the functions indicate the directional orientation of the model. They begin in the top of the core, move to the right to the spiritual life quadrant, then clockwise around the circle to quadrant four. The last three functions reside in the bottom of the core, so that the order of the functions begins and ends in the core.

## THE LEADERSHIP CORE

The first two vital functions reside in the top of the core (C1) within the leadership role. (See Diagram 4A.) Vital function one is leadership, and vital function two is vision/mission. Placing these first two very important functions here has significance. Leaders must initiate. God works in partnership with His leaders and through human instruments.

Please note that the leadership quadrant (C1) contains a function by the same name. This phenomenon occurs three times in the model. It occurs here in the leadership quadrant, in the spiritual life quadrant, and in the ministries quadrant.

## Diagram 4A

### Vital Function One: Leadership

Compare leadership in the church to the functioning of the human mind in the human body. As the mind facilitates all of the functions of the body, so leadership has the responsibility of facilitating the work, health, and growth of the church. Only the mind could acquire by the power of the Spirit the delicate skills needed to facilitate the spiritual life of Christ in His body and each of the other functions. Leadership in church life involves bringing the influence of the mind of Christ upon the church through human instrumentation.

Healthy congregations have effective leaders who understand the leadership function and how it serves God and the church. Effective ministerial leadership stands as one of the most necessary functions within the body of Christ. The genius and skill of leading a congregation to grow requires a strong relationship with Christ, knowledge, experience, and dynamic reflection with a coach or mentor. Knowing what to do, how to do it, and having the courage to reflect on one's practices of leading are premiums for a pastor.

Effective leaders practice self-leadership. They have defined pathways of leadership development so they can lead themselves and others toward maturity in Christ and personal development. Other practitioners have tools they use for the performance of their skills. A pianist uses a piano; an athlete uses the gridiron. The leader, however, uses the self. The apostle Paul compared this self-leadership to training for the race.

> Everyone who competes in the games goes into strict training...I do not run like a man running aimlessly; I do not fight like a man beating the air. No, I beat my body and make it my slave so that after I have preached to others, I myself will not be disqualified for the prize.
>
> —1 CORINTHIANS 9:25–27

Developing the self to become God's quality instrument is a primary focus of the effective church leader.

What does leadership development in the church involve? First, it requires having a defined pathway for development to occur. Church Life utilizes the being, knowing, doing, and reflecting components in its development model. Although these components are generally known, Robert Clinton, in his book *Leadership Emergence Theory,* suggests utilizing these components in leadership training. Clinton points to the work and influence of Fred Holland, specifically Holland's two-track analogy, as resources he integrated into his work using the components of spiritual formation, input, experience, and mentoring.[1]

In Church Life's leadership training, the leader's being must encounter God. The being of a person consists of many components, but these components would definitely include personality, giftings and abilities, callings, personal mission, and character of the person. The being continually molds into the image of Christ as one experiences *yada* (*yāda'*) moments with God, moments of intimate communion and insight. The being fits into God-given roles and develops processes for living and working in the contexts of life.

Second, the leader welcomes continuous knowledge input. Continual and lifelong learning supplies leaders with new information about God, people, the church, themselves, and their contexts. Third, this knowledge is applied to situations. Applying knowledge to situations gives the leader practice in ministry. Knowing whether a particular theory or hunch will work in given situations can only result from trial and error engagement. The fourth component actually ties this process together. The dynamic that includes coaching and/or reflection with mentors maximizes the leadership development process. Here, evaluation and insight mold into learning, making it concrete.

We have utilized this leadership development process for years. We engage it in all of the training environments we lead. This process maximizes learning in the classroom and in multiple settings of ministry. Growth and change occur when the elements of spiritual formation, input, experience, and coaching or mentoring are introduced into training opportunities with leaders.

The dynamic that includes coaching and/or reflection with mentors maximizes the leadership development process.

> Watch your life and doctrine closely. Persevere in them, because if you do, you will save both yourself and your hearers.
>
> —1 Timothy 4:16

**Vital Function Two: Vision/Mission**

Compare the mission and purpose of a local church to the nervous system of the human body. The nervous system consists of the spinal cord and its associated members spread throughout the organism. This system's major responsibility is to initiate, receive, and interpret impulses. Likewise, in the church, these impulses received from the Head—Christ—transmit throughout the church body to bring information and direction. To receive these impulses and to discern these directions require much prayer, communication, testing, and confirmation on the part of the leaders. The leaders of the church must discern the vision, design strategic plans to accomplish the vision, implement the vision with missional goals, and then protect the vision.

Vision/mission discussion always possesses a strange mixture of personal and corporate dynamic. Peter preached in Acts 2:17, taking his text from Joel 2:28–29. He said, "In the last days, God says, I will pour out my Spirit on all people. Your sons and daughters will prophesy, your young men will see visions, your old men will dream dreams." These words imply that persons have the ability to see visions of the work of the kingdom. Both personal vision and church vision, when identified and aligned, provide powerful motivations for fulfillment of the work of the kingdom. Jesus hinted toward this convergence of personal and kingdom vision. He urged New Testament believers to "seek first his kingdom and his righteousness, and all these things will be given to you as well" (Matt. 6:33).

Both personal vision and church vision, when identified and aligned, provide powerful motivations for fulfillment of the work of the kingdom.

The Church Life Model is a missional model, as explained in chapter 3. The quadrants of the model form the vision and missional objectives of the church. Church Life uses a bridge metaphor to depict how the components of vision/mission integrate with the Church Life Model. The vision is the direction of Christ for His church. It provides the motivation to build a bridge into the future. The mission is that part of the vision that the church can reach in the next six months, or the next year for a larger congregation. Some describe this mission as the next level of advancement that the church can reach. The quadrants and core of the Church Life Model form the lanes of the bridge, while strategically planned methodologies give the action steps needed to accomplish the missional goals. Church values and personal values serve as the foundational strength that holds the transformational bridge in place.

Without healthy functioning of vision/mission, the church remains motionless. Lack of movement feels like stagnation, like plateau, or even worse, decline. The system of vision/mission keeps the church advancing. This movement feels like life, like conquest, like victory. The Church Life Model promotes a strong commitment to discerning the mission of God for this church, at this time, in this community. Once the vision and mission are discerned, leaders must initiate movement.

## The Spiritual Life Quadrant

The next three functions make up the first quadrant (Q1) of spiritual life. (See Diagram 4B.) Quadrant one initiates the life of the Spirit within the church. To function properly, the body needs the presence of Christ to energize and sustain it. Although the presence of God must inhabit every nook and cranny of the body, quadrant one promotes igniting this relationship between the people and God. The pastoral leader facilitates this activity. The three vital functions of the spiritual life quadrant are spiritual life, preaching/teaching, and worship. As previously noted, the name of the quadrant is "spiritual life," and it also contains the function of spiritual life.

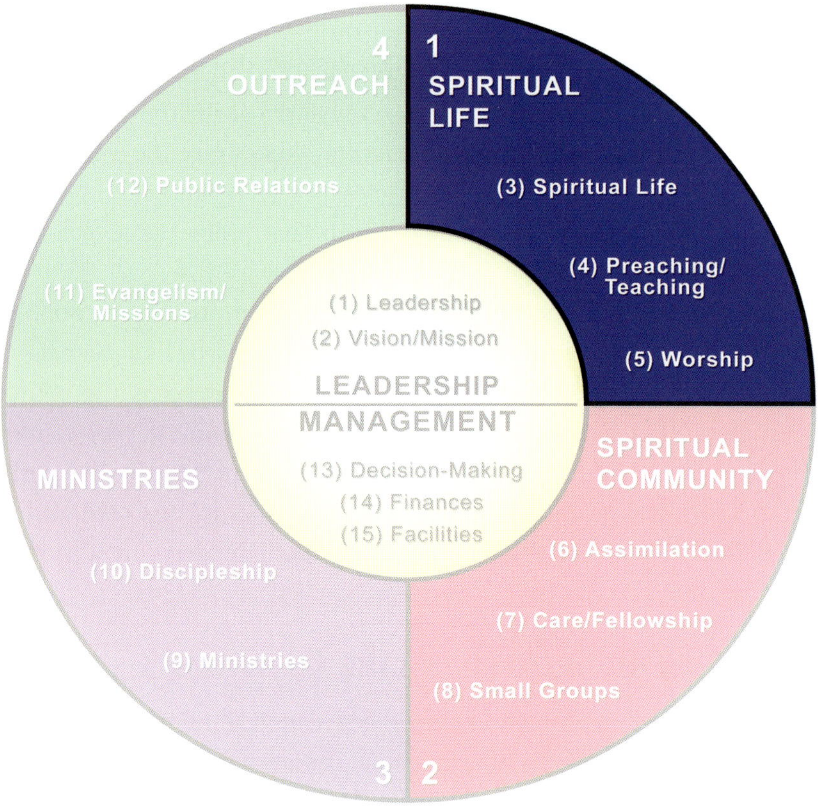


## DIAGRAM 4B

### Vital Function Three: Spiritual Life

Healthy congregations have a balanced, vital, and dynamic spiritual life that gives thrust to the church's mission. Relationship with God, knowing and experiencing Him, certainly serves as the central human motivation of the Christian life and also for participation in the church. However, from the biblical perspective, God not only desires relationship, but He also desires for His people to participate in His mission. As Christ's love for His Father took the form of obedience to God's mission on Earth, He desires this same love from the church. In John 14:31, Jesus said to His disciples, "but the world must learn that I love the Father and that I do exactly what my Father has commanded me." This tension existed for Christ and must exist for the church. The thrust of power that the church experiences as its people abide in relationship with Christ must foster aggressive obedience for mission direction and mission fulfillment.

Healthy persons need a balanced diet that contains recommended proportional servings from all the basic food groups. Such a diet does not mean equal or identical portions of every type of food; rather, it means making wise choices depending on the physical needs of the body and one's lifestyle. A well-balanced natural diet is to the physical body what a balanced spiritual life is to a congregation. A variety of spiritually nurturing activities provides the essentials for a congregation's proper spiritual growth, and these expand as the church grows and its needs evolve. When spiritual growth occurs, spiritual enjoyment increases, but spiritual disciplines must increase as well.

The thrust of power that the church experiences as its people abide in relationship with Christ must foster aggressive obedience for mission direction and mission fulfillment.

The spiritual disciplines of the church serve the body of Christ much like the endocrine system serves the human body. The endocrine system secretes hormones that control organic functions in vital organs and glands, such as the liver, thyroid, and pituitary gland. Likewise, the spiritual life system releases the Spirit of God throughout the body of Christ—the church—giving vitality to its members to meet the needs of the organism and to promote energy for functioning. Spiritual vitality optimizes as members of the body, individually and corporately, enter into spiritual activities and disciplines that bring them into a deeper awareness of God, His presence, and His Word.

Authors such as Dallas Willard and Richard Foster have written exceptional works that assist believers in understanding specific spiritual disciplines and how to practice them.[2] Church Life offers an introductory list of recommended disciplines for the local church:

worship, prayer, Scripture, communication, sacrifice (such as fasting), fellowship, stewardship, ministry service, and submission. We call these disciplines the nine components of spiritual life. Practicing these disciplines individually/privately and then promoting corporate/public practice maximizes spirituality within the church. Early church reformers referred to the disciplines as "means of grace." These varied individual observances serve as the means to connect the believer with God and His people. Likewise, congregations that promote spiritual life observances and activities experience bursts of spiritual life and release a continuous flow of spiritual reality within the church.

> Likewise, the proclamation of the Word in relevant language, content, and style brings vital spiritual nourishment and life to the body of Christ so she can grow, mature, and accomplish the vision and mission of God.

**Vital Function Four: Preaching and Teaching**

Communicating the Word of God to people both inside and outside the congregation is a vital function of the spiritual life quadrant. As noted in the previous section, communication serves as one of the nine components of spiritual life, a discipline that needs constant development. While communication as a discipline represents the broad expression, communicating the Word of God through the vital function of preaching and teaching narrows the goal intensely. This preaching and teaching of the Word centers upon the missional purpose of bringing all persons into an intimate relationship with Jesus Christ so their lives can be changed.

Church Life defines *preaching/teaching* as "communicating the authentic Word of God in a contemporary method with the purpose of changing lives." Remember the words of the apostle Paul, who said, "For Christ did not send me to baptize, but to preach the gospel—not with words of human wisdom, lest the cross of Christ be emptied of its power" (1 Cor. 1:17). Preaching the gospel is about Christ's power changing lives. This life-changing communication called preaching and teaching includes several dimensions. Preaching may aim toward persuading others to serve Christ; it may be evangelistic. Preaching may provoke others toward Christlike actions; it may emphasize morality and behavior. Preaching may reveal truth; it may focus on doctrine.

Healthy congregations place a strong emphasis on this proclamation of the Word. Compare this proclamation in the body of Christ to the circulatory system in the human body. The human circulatory system transports vital nourishment and oxygen to the cells of the body so the body can grow and function with optimum performance. Likewise, the proclamation of the Word in relevant language, content, and style brings vital spiritual nourishment and life to the body of Christ so she can grow, mature, and accomplish the vision and mission of God.

One of the ten values of the Church Life Model introduced in chapter 3 stated the apostolic nature of the model. Because the schema mirrors the New Testament church, we emphasized that it easily accommodates recognition of the role-gifts listed in Ephesians 4. The spiritual life quadrant stands as the home of the prophetic role-gift. Preaching and teaching are prophetic functions; together they declare both the present and future Word from God.

### Vital Function Five: Worship

As noted in the previous discussion of the vital function of spiritual life, worship—both private and public worship—is a spiritual discipline for both the believer and the congregation. In the Church Life Model, worship also serves as a vital function of the spiritual life quadrant.

Healthy congregations have dynamic worship services in which most of the active members participate. Christian Schwarz in *Natural Church Development* states that an "inspiring" worship service "demonstrably separates growing churches from stagnant and declining ones."[3] His study gathered data from one thousand churches from thirty-two countries in six continents to discover those principles that characterize successful churches and could serve as universal principles of health and vitality. "Inspiring worship services" was one of those characteristics. He defines *inspiring* as "an inspiredness which comes from the Spirit of God. Whenever the Holy Spirit is truly at work (and His presence is not merely presumed), He will have a concrete effect upon the way a worship service is conducted including the entire atmosphere of a gathering."[4]

No other experience in the church can compare to this entering into this place of individual and corporate union with the functioning Head of the church.

Meaningful, dynamic worship is to the body of Christ what the respiratory system is to the human body. Basically, the respiratory system interchanges life-giving and life-destroying gases (oxygen and carbon dioxide) for the human body. Similarly, dynamic worship brings the life-giving presence of God into the church while releasing self-destructive, self-centered agendas within the church. Worship, then, serves as the life-flow of Christ to His body. This kind of presence-filled worship refreshes, renews, and energizes individuals and the church as a corporate entity.

Church Life advocates worship that moves participants into a holy of holies, face-to-face encounter with Christ. Worshipers in the Old Testament tabernacle progressed from the outer court of the tabernacle into the holy place and then, ultimately, through the high priest, into the holies of holies to meet with God. The worship experience, if planned well and led by the Holy Spirit, should bring participants face to face with the Lord. The New Testament pictures these believers entering boldly into His presence so they can experience His grace, forgiveness, and strength. No other experience in the church can compare to this entering into this place of individual and corporate union with the functioning Head of the church. Jesus declared to the Samaritan woman in John 4:23, "Yet a time is coming and has now come when the true worshipers will worship the Father in spirit and truth, for they are the kind of worshipers the Father seeks."

As with the preaching and teaching function, worship declares the acts, the works, and the words of God. So, worship is prophetic, and those who participate in worship participate in the role-gift of prophecy. This prophetic worship encourages and edifies participants and announces the acts, works, and words of God to all who hear so they can come to know Him.

In summary, the spiritual life quadrant provides a home for the functions of spiritual life, preaching and teaching, and worship. This home sets an atmosphere of rich spiritual intimacy with God through personal devotion as well as private and public participation in the disciplines. It is a place where preaching and teaching nourish the body with the Word and a place where presence-filled worship strengthens hearts; it is a place where the prophetic gifts proclaim the wonderful ways and works of mighty God.

## The Spiritual Community Quadrant

Moving clockwise around the model, the next missional quadrant bears the name "spiritual community" (Q2). This quadrant provides a home for the functions of assimilation, care and fellowship, and small groups. (See Diagram 4C.) While quadrant one connects people to God, quadrant two connects people to one another. This second movement gathers the believers in *koinonia* fellowship, a fellowship of intimacy together with God, in His face and sight.

People choose to attend churches for many different reasons. Perhaps the prophetic preaching, the inspiring worship, or a particular missional outreach event will draw a person into the congregation. However, it is this missional quadrant of the church, the spiritual community, that provides the glue to hold believers in the fellowship. Attendees become members when the spiritual community welcomes them and provides a sanctuary of care and fellowship.

To belong to the family of God trumps most other attractive features of the church. To belong to the family of God meets a deep emotional and spiritual need of human beings. To belong to the family of God provides the privilege to participate in the *koinonia* presence of God. This presence is as real and wonderful as the presence that fills the sanctuary where worship and preaching occur. This presence surrounds, envelops, and acknowledges the individual uniqueness of each person. Yet, this Presence makes the body one in Christ's love.

> To belong to the family of God trumps most other attractive features of the church. To belong to the family of God meets a deep emotional and spiritual need of human beings.

Integration of the processes of the individual functions occurs within each of the quadrants. However, no quadrant demonstrates this integration and dependency more apparently than the spiritual community quadrant. Each function depends heavily upon the others for effectiveness. Assimilation needs the systems of care and fellowship and small groups to successfully integrate visitors into the community. Likewise, care and fellowship and small groups function well when the assimilation process provides new persons for their groups and for their care systems. This truth will become more evident as explanations are given for these functions.

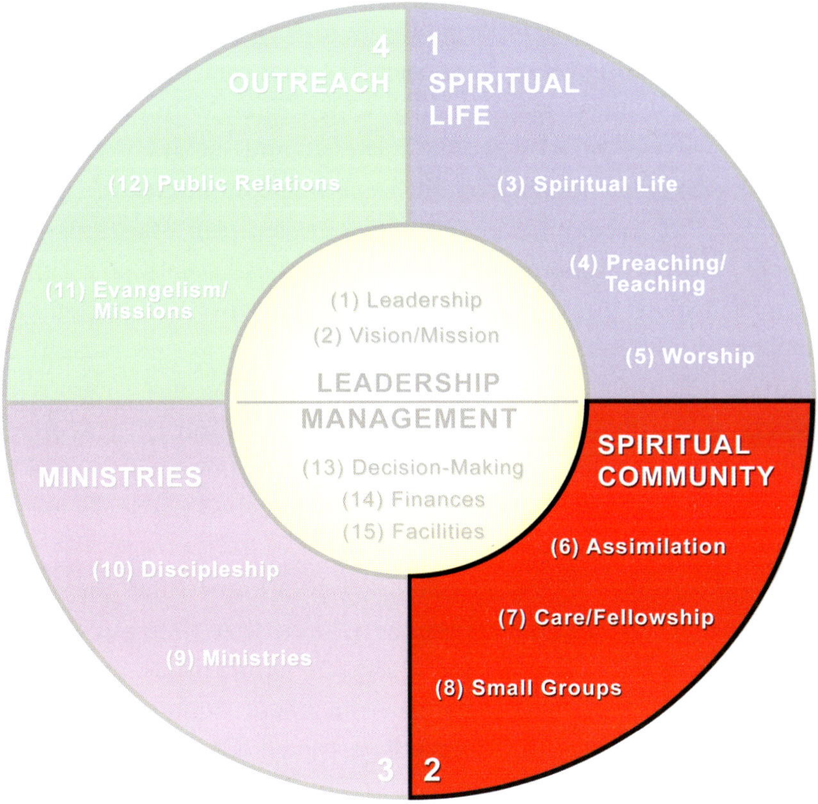


## Diagram 4C

### Vital Function Six: Assimilation

Assimilation is the sixth vital function of the Church Life Model. It is the system that connects people, families, and people groups to the local church and then integrates them into the spiritual community. The process of assimilation serves to attach those gained from evangelism efforts, those attracted to the ministries of the church, and those transitioning from other churches. Healthy congregations have an effective plan for incorporating these newcomers, new believers, and new members into the life of the church.

Compare the assimilation system to the sensory devices of the human body, such as the olfactory nerve that relates to the sense of smell. The sensory system keeps the human body aware of external realities. The sensory functions keep external and internal realities connected and integrated. Similarly, Christ intended for His church to become aware of, to welcome, relate to, and integrate those new persons who come in contact with the church community.

Church Life recommends a simple, four-step plan of assimilation: (1) offer targeted, attractive ministry and relational events, (2) establish communication through several different means with those new persons who attend, (3) assign a trained sponsor to new persons or families, (4) move the new persons into small group environs as quickly as possible. Smaller congregations assimilate all newcomers within this one-track plan. The larger congregations will choose to have streamlined plans for visitors based upon their particular needs for spiritual community.

> Churches with open hearts of welcome grow and add daily to their spiritual community.

Some visitors know when they walk into the church that they are looking for a church home; these are potential new members. Some visitors have recently accepted Christ and wish to receive teaching and discipleship; these are potential new believers needing discipleship. Other visitors attend to "try out" the church to see if they can find friends; these are newcomers looking for relationship. Congregations who can target these different visitor needs will find success in assimilating new people into their community. Targeting these needs involves providing individual tracks for visitors seeking relationship by assigning trained sponsors who understand their relational needs and by offering a small group specifically designed for them, e.g. a newcomer's fellowship. Similarly, those looking for a church home need a trained sponsor who understands membership in the church and who can help them assimilate into a new member's small group.

*Connection* and *integration* are the key words in assimilation. The Church Life Model fosters strong spiritual community and encourages an effective process of assimilation so that new converts are added daily to the church. Churches with open hearts of welcome grow and add daily to their spiritual community. Luke tells us that New Testament believers developed this process of assimilation. In Acts 2:44, he reports, "All the believers were together and had everything in common." He continues in verse 47, "And the Lord added to their number daily those who were being saved."

### Vital Function Seven: Care and Fellowship

When a church's care system functions effectively, each person in the community receives quality care. Only a system of care can provide the comfort, prayer, encouragement, and kindness needed by members of a church community. Care is the responsibility of the members of the church. In 2 Corinthians 1:3–4, the writer acknowledges the Father as "the Father of compassion and the God of all comfort, who comforts us in all our troubles, so that we can comfort those in any trouble with the comfort we ourselves have received from God." Father God expects His people to comfort one another and care for another. Scriptures teach that members of the spiritual family must love one another, care for one another, and bear one another's burdens.

> Only a system of care can provide the comfort, prayer, encouragement, and kindness needed by members of a church community. Care is the responsibility of the members of the church.

Healthy congregations have a significant number of caring individuals or groups who provide relational care and bonding within the congregation. Compare this caring system within the body of Christ to the epithelial system of the human body. This is the outer tissue covering of the body that provides continuous connection of body tissues and protects the organism. Similarly, caring relationships within the relational network of the church cover and protect the individual members of the body of Christ.

The Church Life Model promotes a connected group of caregivers that invades every small group of the community. This person may be called the caregiver or the hospitality person. Regardless of the title, this trained caregiver senses the needs of individuals in the small group and provides quality care for them. A trained caregiver knows how to serve and how to contact other caregivers, such as pastoral staff, for assistance when needed. Caregivers also provide care for specialized areas, such as for the dying, grieving, poor, or hurting.

Not all persons in the body can receive direct, primary care from the pastor, but he must care for the leaders who serve the spiritual community with him. Layers of care responsibility ensure that members of the core (the committed), members of the congregation (the regular attendees), and members of the larger community (the occasional attendees) receive quality care and comfort.

### Vital Function Eight: Small Groups

The Church Life function of small groups promotes the necessity of relationships in the spiritual community. Jesus accentuated relationship with God as the first commandment. He gave the second commandment in the same setting—one must establish relationship with one's fellow sojourners (Matt. 22:37–40). Relationships are the "bones" and "joints" or glue that hold the body of Christ together. God uses these relational structures for individual placement, protection, and function.

> From him the whole body, joined and held together by every supporting ligament, grows and builds itself up in love, as each part does its work.
>
> —EPHESIANS 4:16

Healthy, growing congregations have developed a system to relationally connect the members of the body of Christ through small groups. This small group function contributes significantly to all of the systems of quadrant two, spiritual community, and provides the group framework for the systems of ministries, discipleship, and outreach as well. Just as the skeletal system of the body provides structure and support for the vital organs of the body, likewise, small groups provide an internal framework that connects the spiritual gifts and energy of the members together so the body can grow in Christ, be nurtured, and expand in ministry effectiveness.

When some leaders think of small groups, they immediately think of a program or a separate ministry within the church. Envisioning small groups as smaller units of relational networks existing in the body will help members to realize the basic and true nature of the small group system. A loose structuring of these units creates the first framework of this vital function. In the smaller congregation, these units of relationship may exist as basic ministries and task groups. As the church grows, the need for other multiple connections and ministry points will evolve.

The Church Life Model envisions a system of small groups that provides multiple ministry leadership roles, meets in homes, accomplishes ministry together, offers accountability, encourages spiritual growth, assimilates new persons, and encourages participation in the spiritual community. Multiple leadership roles give opportunity for congregants to exercise their spiritual gifts. Meeting in homes mirrors the New Testament behavior of believers. Accomplishing ministry together builds momentum for vision and mission fulfillment. The accountability and nurture provided by small groups mature believers and encourage their spiritual growth. Perhaps the strongest contribution of small groups is providing a place for people to participate and belong.

Envisioning small groups as smaller units of relational networks existing in the body will help members to realize the basic and true nature of the small group system.

The need to belong transcends culture and time; it is a universal need. Even in contemporary culture, electronic small groups emerge from the relational dysfunction of sterile individualism. Blogs, chat rooms, Facebook, and texting have grown from the need to connect and belong. Human beings need relationships, even relationships with no person-to-person physical contact. Some will settle for only these electronic relationships. It is our opinion, however, that these contacts provide shallow pathways for the spiritual life of God to travel among His people, and to those who are not yet His people. New Testament Christians and contemporary Christians in certain countries risk their lives daily to meet in spiritual community with God. The small groups system serves the Church Life Model as a vital function of the spiritual community quadrant, providing opportunities for connection and relational intimacy.

The need to belong transcends culture and time; it is a universal need. Even in contemporary culture, electronic small groups emerge from the relational dysfunction of sterile individualism.

## THE MINISTRIES QUADRANT

Moving farther clockwise and upward around the model, the next missional quadrant bears the name "ministries" (Q3). This quadrant provides a home for the functions of ministries and discipleship. (See Diagram 4D.) While quadrant one connects people to God and quadrant two connects people to one another, this third movement provides the opportunity for believers to both receive and give ministry. Also, the system of discipleship exists to give prominent attention to the growth and maturity of members.

Believers mature in Christ through multiple means—encounters with God, hearing and receiving the Word, exercising spiritual gifts, involvement in ministry within the church, and involvement in ministry toward those who need to hear and experience the love and power of God. Becoming like Christ must be the main preoccupation of the believer—the goal of every Christian. The ministries quadrant, with its systems of ministries and discipleship, focuses the spiritual and human energy of the church toward this goal. The role-gift of teacher operates most actively in this quadrant.

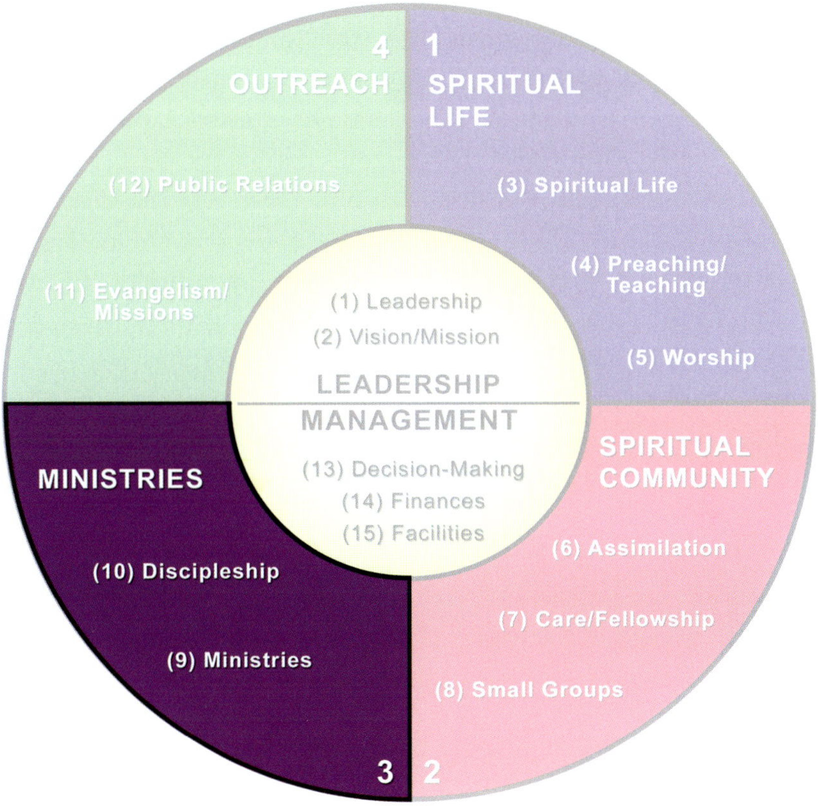


## Diagram 4D

### Vital Function Nine: Ministries

Vital function nine of the Church Life Model is ministries. Healthy congregations have a strong infrastructure of laity-led ministries that mobilize the laity to fulfill the mission of the organism. In the human body, the skeletal system gives form and support to the vital organs and muscles. This structure either releases the body to grow or restricts its growth. Lay leadership structures, in a similar way, provide the support for the natural growth of the church. They either release and facilitate church growth or inhibit it.

The Great Commission of Christ motivates the ministries system as well as its counterpart, the discipleship system. The words of Jesus move leaders and laity alike: "Therefore go and *make disciples... teaching them* to obey everything I have commanded you" (Matt. 28:19–20, emphasis added). Most church ministries purport that their activities within the church and community qualify as this ministry commanded by Christ. Because these activities find their origins in Scripture, the common belief prevails that any practice of these activities through ministry programs is the ministry of Christ. These programs are often "canned" approaches borrowed from other successful ministries in other churches in other locations.

Ray Anderson, a noted practical theologian, asserts that ministry qualifies as God's ministry if "determined and set forth by God's own ministry of revelation and reconciliation in the world, beginning with Israel and culminating in Jesus Christ and the church."[5] He points to the fact that even Jesus did not engage in ministry determined by Himself or even human need but a ministry of reconciliation determined by the will of the Father.

> The ministries system of the church houses the precious commodity of God's ministry, the only ministry that should exist.

Through the ministry of the Holy Spirit, the doing of ministry unites with God's ministry accomplished in Christ. Anderson writes, "Ministry is God's way of reaffirming and expounding the truth of who God is and what God wishes to reveal through what he has said and done.... Every act of ministry reveals something of God."[6]

Avoiding canned, piecemeal ministry programs will bring leaders to the task of discovering the present ministry activity of Christ within the church. The next step involves discerning the ministries that God desires to initiate. Jesus stated clearly in John 5:19, "I tell you the truth, the Son can do nothing by himself; he can do only what he sees his Father doing, because whatever the Father does the Son also does." Leaders must ask, What ministry does the Father desire for this church? What partnership of ministry does God want us to participate in at this time with these people in this context? Once these questions are asked and answered, then leaders must build these ministries from the foundations. The phases of this ministry building include recognizing the vision and values, establishing the goals and priorities, identifying the training content for the leaders, selecting the gifted personnel, developing a program, and providing the atmosphere or ambiance needed for the ministry.

Much prayer and careful planning should attend the process of ministry planning and initiation. Regular evaluation of the ministry's effectiveness and personnel must occur as well. Keeping ministry squarely in the center of God's ministry in the world and not allowing human agenda or human need to push activities toward some other mission or goal requires frequent, honest evaluation. The ministries system of the church houses the precious commodity of God's ministry, the only ministry that should exist.

**Vital Function Ten: Discipleship**

Vital function ten of the Church Life Model is discipleship. Healthy, growing congregations have developed systems of discipleship. Compare discipleship in the church body to the muscular system of the human body. This muscular system is composed of ligaments and tendons that provide connectedness, flexibility, strength, and mobility for the body. Likewise, the discipleship ministry promotes growth and establishes strength within the members so that the body moves, grows, and fulfills the vision and mission of God.

> Can the discipler lead disciples to a place of encounter so they can know God intimately and be formed into His likeness? This component may not only be the qualifying component of discipleship but also of leadership in the church.

"I am forty-five years old. I have been in the church all my life, and I have served as a church leader for the past fifteen years. This is the first time anyone has attempted to disciple me." These words came from a prominent leader in a large suburban church we pastored. Many similar words have been spoken in many settings as we struggled to fulfill the Great Commission of Jesus among His people and churches. The Great Discipler spoke to His own chosen disciples in John 14–16, instructing them in the basics of the discipleship experience. He teaches them about love, truth, obedience, suffering, abiding, and fruitfulness. In John 15:8 Jesus says, "This is to my Father's glory, that you bear much fruit, showing yourselves to be my disciples." Isn't this Christ's expected outcome for His disciples? For one to participate in being a disciple and in making new disciples appears to be the goal and mission that Jesus had in mind. He even added the clincher that the Father is glorified in this fruit-bearing. This fruit-bearing is most likely producing the spiritual fruit of Christ's own nature (maturity) and the spiritual fruit of "making disciples" (multiplication).

Most authors agree that the goal or mission of discipleship is to make disciples—teach, train, and equip them—so they in turn can fulfill the Great Commission to make disciples also. Contemporary leaders and churches have the responsibility to define this process for present church constituents. Church Life advocates a discipleship process with movement from initial, new believer training that emphasizes "becoming a disciple" to "becoming a discipler." Churches may title their layers and stages according to their needs and contexts. Church Life advocates an entrance level and an advanced level. The entrance level follows the general movement of the Church Life Model with emphasis on commitment to Christ, commitment to community, commitment to ministry, and commitment to the church. The advanced level follows a more in-depth approach for committed followers to grow in relationship with Christ, grow in ministry influence, grow in ministry effectiveness, and grow in kingdom fruitfulness.

The defining component of discipleship in Church Life lies in the ingredient of knowing God, "encountering" Him. Can the discipler lead disciples to a place of encounter so they can know God intimately and be formed into His likeness? This component may not only be the qualifying component of discipleship but also of leadership in the church.

The Old Testament indicates intimate relationship encounter with God using the Hebrew word *yada* (*yāda*ʿ), meaning to experience God. The New Testament renders to know as *ginosko* (*ginōskō*), meaning to respond to Him, to interact with Him, to become like Him, as well as to learn about Him. John 1:18 declares that no one has seen God. If God cannot be seen, then how can one know God? He is made known through Jesus Christ. So through knowing Christ, New Testament believers can know God, just as the Old Testament believers knew God. First John 2:3–6 ties knowledge of God to response toward Him to conform to the image of God.

> We know that we have come to know him if we obey his commands. The man who says, "I know him," but does not do what he commands is a liar, and the truth is not in him. But if anyone obeys his word, God's love is truly made complete in him. This is how we know we are in him: Whoever claims to live in him must walk as Jesus did.

Leading disciples into the devotional activities of prayer, contemplation, and observance of the disciplines will assist in spiritual formation. Leaders must create these and other pathways of discipleship for themselves and for members of the church. Thus, the system of discipleship is a vital function and process of the Church Life Model.

## The Outreach Quadrant

The final missional quadrant of the Church Life Model is the outreach quadrant (Q4), shown in Diagram 4E. This final missional quadrant, named the outreach quadrant, contains the functions of evangelism/missions and public relations. The role-gift of evangelist prospers in the outreach quadrant and these two functions.

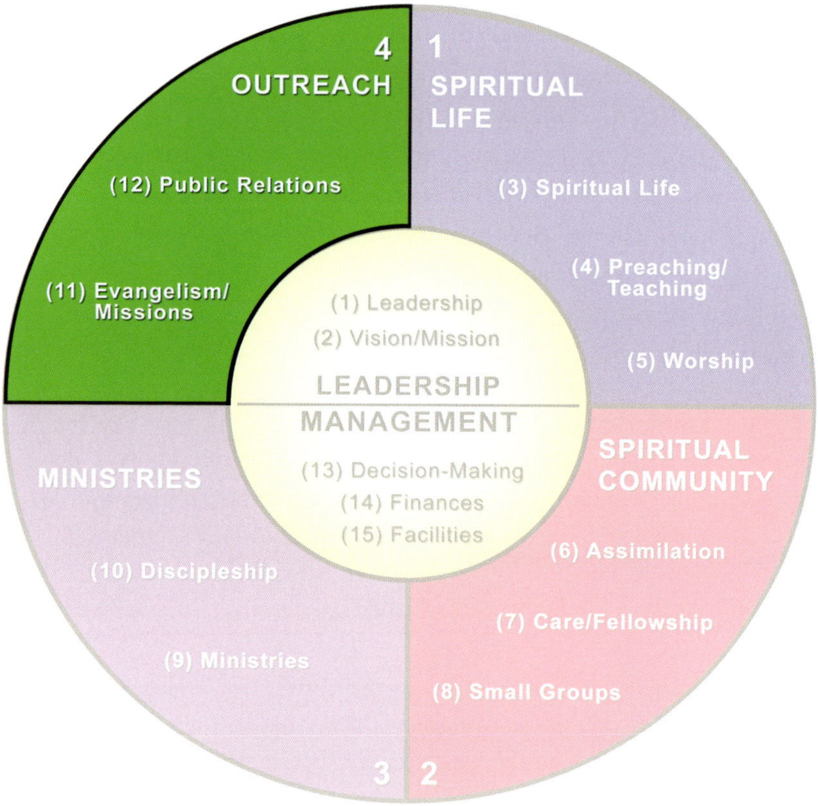


## DIAGRAM 4E

### Vital Function Eleven: Evangelism and Missions

The function of evangelism/missions centers in the mandate of the Great Commission. Whereas the vital functions of ministries and discipleship center upon the teaching and encounter aspects of the Great Commission, evangelism and missions focus upon the "going" aspects. Here the church finds its place as the agent of the kingdom to invade its communities with the gospel message. Each church has potential to win those certain individuals in its localities, in its cultural environments, and in its specific harvests. Reaching these persons forms the agenda of the function of evangelism/missions.

Healthy, vibrant congregations seek new, receptive groups of people through their evangelistic initiatives. This compares well to the reproductive system of the human body. This system provides for the continuation of the species. The continued growth, fulfillment, and joy of the local church rest upon the accomplishment of the congregation's evangelistic movements.

> The New Testament orients signs, wonders, and many of the spiritual gifts within the evangelism context of the world, the field, and the marketplace.

Some churches limit this function to missions activities. Missions activities to certain countries, certain cultures, and to certain need groups are not an option for the church. In fact, Jesus did not mince words in Matthew 25:34–46. He clearly stated His expectations—those whom He knows will feed the hungry, give drink to the thirsty, offer lodging to the stranger, clothe the poor, care for the sick, and visit the imprisoned. These activities are required. However, do these caring actions qualify as evangelism, reaching one's own cultures with the gospel message?

Church Life advocates an evangelism emphasis outside the church in the "field." From observation, it appears that churches often wait for new persons to arrive on their doorsteps. Also, very few of the churches' resources make their way into the main mission that Christ accentuated, going outside the church and into the world to preach the gospel and disciple. This evangelism activity is not a one-time event but a planned process that targets pre-Christians with defined stages of evangelism. The stages recommended by Church Life derive from the concepts of C. Peter Wagner, who advocated three broad approaches: establishing the presence of God, proclaiming the gospel, and persuasion to salvation.[7] The processes within each stage prove crucial, as well as the types and methods of evangelism utilized. Each context demands a customized strategy for its targeted groups.

Quickly, however, the evident fact emerges that while stages, processes, methods, and strategies align with the mission and direction of evangelism, these efforts alone cannot provide the spiritual power for the work nor produce spiritual life in the hearts of the recipients. This life comes only from God. A marriage ceremony brings a man and woman together, but only God can produce life from the union. A seed can be planted, but only God can cause life to grow from it. Likewise, He promises that if we go in His name, He will accompany us with His presence and His powerful Holy Spirit. He declares at the end of the words of the Great Commission, "And surely I am with you" (Matt. 28:20). Again, in the commission of Mark 16:17, He assures the disciples that "signs will accompany those who believe." In His last words of Luke 24:49 and Acts 1:8, Jesus clearly instructs the disciples to wait for the spiritual power necessary to make their evangelism efforts fruitful.

The evangelism function occurs in the marketplace, in the field. This function exudes the power gifts. The New Testament orients signs, wonders, and many of the spiritual gifts within the evangelism context of the world, the field, and the marketplace. Herein lay the presence and the power for mission fulfillment. Just as Christ revealed God to the world through demonstrations resulting in many believers, so the church as the agent of Christ in the world must go with the spiritual power to bring His presence, to proclaim His message, and to persuade men and women to follow Christ.

### Vital Function Twelve: Public Relations

The public relations function has two distinct audiences. Most churches focus the majority of their time, energy, and financial resources on the internal audience, persons within the church. The external audience, potential constituents within the local context, needs a planned strategy of consistent communication as well. Churches need a balanced approach of public relations directed toward both of these groups.

Compare the public relations function of the church to the sense organs of the human body. The common five senses are sight, smell, taste, feeling, and hearing. However, human beings can also sense balance, motion, pain, barometric pressure, and a supernatural presence. When planning public relations, leaders must sense those ministries or media methods that give the church maximum visibility and accessibility with both its internal audience and its external audience. Healthy congregations are known in their communities because of their excellent leaders, quality ministries, and visible locations.

A biblical view of the pastoral role asks that the pastor envision both the internal and external communities as his pastoral responsibility. We often communicate to pastors that they are sent to pastor the church, and the community through the church. This perspective adopts the posture that the church exists as the agent of the kingdom in the world to bring light, salvation, and transformation to all within its reach.

A biblical view of the pastoral role asks that the pastor envision both the internal and external communities as his pastoral responsibility.

Some churches are practically invisible to anyone other than its members. Such a church exists but has no identity. Having an identity and a good reputation in the community comes with a price tag. The church must forsake isolationism, minister to both human and spiritual needs within the community, foster multiple points of entry into the church, and seek to minister to persons in the community during times of crises and transition. A good public relations approach develops creative ways to pierce the darkness with the light of the gospel and overcome the blindness and resistance of persons in the community. Paul, speaking by the Spirit, informs us, "The god of this age has blinded the minds of unbelievers, so that they cannot see the light of the gospel of the glory of Christ, who is the image of God" (2 Cor. 4:4).

Remember, the role-gift of evangelism finds full expression in both functions of the outreach quadrant, evangelism/missions and public relations. Perceiving public relations as a function energized by the spiritual gift of evangelism assists in understanding the true nature of this system in the Church Life Model.

Church Life suggests detailed plans and a budget for creating excellent public relations internally and externally. Choosing the most effective methods of internal and external communication consumes the largest portion of this planning. Establishing clear communication and good public relations with those both inside and outside the church forms the agenda of the public relations function of Church Life.

> Having an identity and a good reputation in the community comes with a price tag.

The outreach quadrant (Q4) is the last of the missional quadrants. This discussion of the fifteen vital functions has continued in a clockwise movement all the way around the Church Life Model. The final movement takes us back again to the inside of the core and into the bottom half of the inner circle, into the management core (C2).

## THE MANAGEMENT CORE

As stated at the beginning of this cursory look into the fifteen vital functions, the central core of the Church Life Model contains two divisions—the top of the core (C1) and the bottom of the core (C2). Situated in the top of the core is the role of leadership, while the management role occupies the bottom of the core. These dual roles of leadership and management intersect with each of the quadrants and reflect two sides of one coin—leaders lead, then they manage. As mentioned previously, the leadership and management roles mirror the role-gift of the apostle.

Just as effectiveness determines the health of the leadership role, efficiency determines the health of the management role. Both have equal impact upon the health of the church, and each of the ministry quadrants needs both leadership and management direction from the leaders of the church. While management aims toward efficiency, this role also gives priority attention to quality. The vital functions of decision-making, finances, and facilities find their places in the management core, as shown in Diagram 4F.

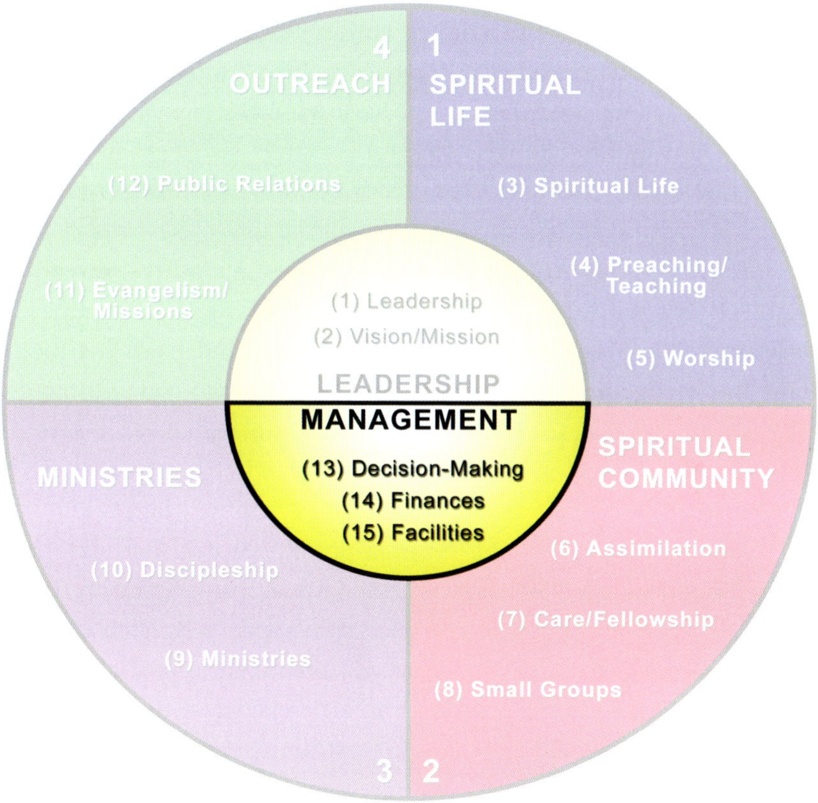


## Diagram 4F

### Vital Function Thirteen: Decision-Making

Compare decision-making in the church to the immune system of the human body. This system protects from harmful bacteria or viruses that potentially hurt or disable the human body. In the same manner, the decision-making function of the local church provides a pathway to process healthy decisions, manage potential conflicts, or initiate needed change.

> The management function needs a process of decision-making to ensure sound and wise decisions.

Pastors contend with a volume of

daily decisions that do not wait. Problems continually cascade toward the leaders. The reality of change rushes toward the contemporary church almost uncontrollably. Preventing these realities is impossible. Instead, the leader identifies a process to facilitate decisions, manage conflicts, and guide change as a constructive way to manage these realities. If quality decisions can occur about 95 percent of the time, problems can find resolution before escalating into crises, and changes can occur without losing constituents. The Scriptures reveal the origin of this wisdom needed in decision-making. In Proverbs 2:6, Scripture states, "For the LORD gives wisdom, and from his mouth come knowledge and understanding." James, in the New Testament, instructs us in what to do when wisdom is unavailable. He says, "If any of you lacks wisdom, he should ask God, who gives generously to all without finding fault, and it will be given to him" (James 1:5).

The management function needs a process of decision-making to ensure sound and wise decisions. After researching literature in the field of decision-making, Church Life settled upon a six-step decision-making process: (1) define the issue; (2) identify the participants; (3) collect and assess related information; (4) consider options and risks; (5) obtain action agreements; and (6) test, implement, and communicate the decision. Healthy, well-managed congregations have a streamlined, participative decision-making structure within the church body. Such a system helps sustain the natural health and growth of the church.

> Although good financial principles from other sources provide wise counsel, priority counsel for the church emanates from the Scriptures.

Most contemporary church authorities list conflict as a major cause of church dysfunction, plateau, and decline in America. Seedbeds where these conflicts and relational difficulties grow include the areas of governance, vision, mission, values, methodologies, and change. Having a decision-making system that guides both major church decisions as well as decisions in every governance group will increase the possibility of proper functioning within the body.

**Vital Function Fourteen: Finances**

The financial system of the church, vital function fourteen, provides the resources to maintain adequate personnel, ministry programs, and facilities. In the body of Christ, financial resources must convert into the fuel required to maintain the health and growth of the church. Compare the financial system to the digestive system in the human body, which converts food substances into nutrients so the body can thrive and grow.

Jesus addressed the issue of financial resources frequently in His teachings. Therefore, healthy congregations concern themselves with a biblical perspective of the financial resources of the people and the church. Although good financial principles from other sources provide wise counsel, priority counsel for the church emanates from the Scriptures.

The first priority of any financial system involves commitment to integrity and accountability. Pastors of healthy congregations commit to conduct all of the financial affairs of the church in a manner that honors God and meets all laws governing the body. Integrity is a heart value that the leadership team of the local church must embrace.

Church Life draws several principles directly from the teachings of Jesus about stewardship of money. Matthew 25:14–30, the parable of the talents, gives several broad concepts that form the foundation of the financial system of the kingdom. Those broad principles include (1) all the earth and its resources belong to God, who entrusts those resources to people; (2) God gives differing amounts of resources; (3) individuals must utilize resources to produce resources; (4) God expects wise stewardship; (5) He adds resources to wise stewards and removes resources from unwise stewards. These

> Building a culture of generosity requires acts of generosity, just as a church builds a culture of care through acts of caring.

words of Jesus encourage responsibility for the use of money, both individually and corporately.

The apostle Paul wrote much about the attitude that should prevail in the function of finances within the church. He uses the words *generously* and *cheerfully* in 2 Corinthians 9:6–15. Generosity does not automatically occur within a church; the people must cultivate this attitude. Building a culture of generosity requires acts of generosity, just as a church builds a culture of care through acts of caring. Church Life promotes generous giving by assisting leaders in cultivating the financial resources of the church. Again, these principles must emanate from Scripture. Some of these principles include the following: God's provisions follow His purposes, sowing and reaping, and prayer for partners.

In order to maintain adequate personnel, ministry programs, and facilities, the local church needs sufficient financial resources. Church Life advocates that churches adopt a biblical view of stewardship and establish good principles and processes so the church can properly cultivate and manage its financial systems.

### Vital Function Fifteen: Facilities

The last of the functions is facilities, vital function fifteen. Healthy congregations provide appropriate facilities and adequate parking for their constituents. Church Life is not the first to compare the physical facilities of the church to the clothing needed for the human body. As most would agree, clothes are a necessity and also make a statement about the person wearing the clothes. Beyond serving as covering for the body, clothes indicate image, size, age, style, and perhaps attitude. Likewise, the physical facilities of a church reflect its personality and ministries.

Practitioners and theologians do not agree about the necessity of facilities. Some argue that New Testament believers met in the temple and in homes. House churches flourish in many cultures where facilities are scarce. American churches often overbuild facilities and bring embarrassment to their members. Others advocate that the essence of the church forms when the people meet; therefore, church buildings prove unnecessary. It appears evident from the history of the church that physical facilities memorialize the work of God in an area. When God works among a group of people, a resulting physical representation of that spiritual reality emerges. Though God's greatest work occurs in the human spirit, He also provides mankind with works that declare His glory as well.

The facilities function of Church Life advocates adequate and appropriate facilities for the body. Because building facilities has surfaced as such a sensitive issue, church leaders should take the time to examine biblical accounts of those building projects conducted in the Old Testament. (See Exodus 35–40; 1 Chronicles 22–29; Ezra 3–6; and Nehemiah 1–6.) Principles will emerge from these projects that can guide the present process of building a house for the people of God. Church Life promotes some of these basic principles, such as having a master plan, selecting a builder, and planning the appropriate spaces needed.

Some churches succeed in constructing striking edifices on beautiful grounds, only to discover that they have neglected to build the body at the same time. Losing momentum in ministry and movement toward vision can sabotage the most well-developed plans for church advancement and growth. Church Life suggests construction of a church advancement plan to coincide with the building plan of the church. This plan helps to ensure that the essence of the church, the people of God, remains healthy and functioning well so they can inhabit the new facility with strength and purpose.

Some churches succeed in constructing striking edifices on beautiful grounds, only to discover that they have neglected to build the body at the same time.

This chapter has taken readers on a journey through the fifteen vital functions of the Church Life Model. The journey has defined each function and given a brief glimpse into some of the principles operative for each of those systems. General points of understanding about the nature of each of the four quadrants and the two sections of the core of the framework have been discussed. This completes the task of defining the basic components of the model. Our discussion of the Church Life Model will now progress to suggestions of ways to engage the paradigm in the local church.

# 5

# WHAT PATTERNS WORK BEST WHEN ENGAGING THE MODEL?

*Therefore, since we are surrounded by such a great cloud of witnesses, let us throw off everything that hinders and the sin that so easily entangles, and let us run with perseverance the race marked out for us.*

—Hebrews 12:1

ACTIVITIES SURROUNDING A particular congregation's engagement of the Church Life Model in its local environment will differ significantly from church to church. Many variables and idiosyncrasies exist within each church's unique DNA and context. This individuality of the body requires each church to formulate a customized plan of engagement fitting its own particular personality and situation. However, certain patterns or basic movements have materialized as churches have connected with the essential components of the model. These patterns, discussed in the following paragraphs, can assist leaders in the process of connecting.

This chapter suggests patterns for connecting an existing church with the Church Life paradigm. First the commentary will highlight the larger global engagement assumptions. Then more specific patterns will pinpoint some detailed engagement behaviors that pastors and church leaders can utilize.

The second part of the chapter will consider the value of the Church Life Function Assessment for the initiatory stages of convergence. A conversation about the assessment will consider its components, address its usefulness for evaluating the strengths and weaknesses of the systems of the church, and comment on its reliability and validity. All of these topics will add greatly to the discourse of this section. The chapter will end with discussion of the composite assessment drawn from our Church Life Function Assessment database files, representing input from over eleven hundred churches and over six thousand assessments.

> Become so familiar with the model that you can explain it to others as a simple physical paradigm representing the spiritual reality of the church.

## Global Engagement Principles

The global principles of engagement assist church leaders with knowing where to begin. They are not steps but principles from which to initiate behaviors. Read through this section not with a linear mind-set but with the goal of understanding some of the possible patterns for engaging the Church Life Model within the local setting. The words of this section are easy to remember—*memorize, visualize, personalize,* and *strategize.*

**Memorize: Engage the Church Life Model as a mental model first.**

Begin by memorizing the individual components, the colors, and the names of the core and quadrants. Commit to memory the fifteen vital functions and their location in each major pastoral role (missional quadrant). While memorizing, try to discern the spiritual and developmental movement the model promotes. This movement draws people into relationship with God and into relationship with others.

Then, it connects people in groups so the giftings of each person can impact others for Christ both inside and outside the church. Discern the flow of mission in the framework.

Become so familiar with the model that you can draw it quickly and insert all the components in record time. Become so familiar with it that you can converse easily with others about the model, referring to the systems and the quadrants with ease. Become so familiar with the model that you can explain it to others as a simple physical paradigm representing the spiritual reality of the church. Make the model familiar, owning it and making it yours by memorizing it.

**Visualize: Use the model as a lens to view the components of the existing church.**

Place the Church Life framework over the existing church and view the present church through the lens of the Church Life Model. Begin locating the systems and their parts, however presently configured. Fit the common pieces together. Each body will have some uniqueness, but all of the systems will exist in every church. Those systems may appear in only bits and pieces, some functional and some dysfunctional. Gather the pieces of each system together and note the way that each functions in the existing organism.

Each body will have some uniqueness, but all of the systems will exist in every church.

Each functional system and its missional quadrant provide windows of meaning and mission within the congregation. People group around and within these systems depending upon their spiritual giftedness and callings. Find these groups; search for the functions. If one can identify the present components of the existing church within the framework, then the church can engage the model by personalizing the components.

**Personalize: Own the model for the existing congregation.**

Making the model one's own for the existing church brings the highest degree of personalization and ownership. This work takes time. Do not suppose that this engaging task must be completed before progressing to more specific engagement behaviors. Though personalizing the model proves difficult initial work, the process accentuates the organic nature of both the church and the model. The existing church does not cram itself into a mold called a model. This would treat the model as a rigid, confining, and organizational mold, unusable for the living organism. Rather, the church and the model intersect, integrate, adapt, and morph into one another toward alignment with biblical principles, movement toward spiritual mission, and refreshment of spiritual presence.

The model provides the basic structure for the church by strong adherence to the designs given in Scripture. These theological foundations were discussed in earlier chapters. They include the truth that Jesus is the Head of the church, and the members are the individual parts. They include recognition of the mandates given to first-century believers—the mandates called the Great Commandment and Great Commission. The church now congeals around those basic principles just as flesh and sinew form around the skeleton of the human body. This personalizing yields into a new, soft entity with formable components ready for growth and movement.

The existing church does not cram itself into a mold called a model. This would treat the model as a rigid, confining, and organizational mold, unusable for the living organism.

An outcome of this work could result in the names for the missional quadrants becoming names the congregation can own, value, and promote. These words should define the unique mission of the church in all four quadrants. So, the Church Life Model utilized by a church may morph into different words of mission for each church. One congregation used alliterative words for their quadrant names, as shown in Diagram 5A.

| Missional Quadrant | Church Life Quadrant Name | Church Name for Missional Quadrant |
|---|---|---|
| Quadrant One | Spiritual Life | Exalt |
| Quadrant Two | Community Life | Embrace |
| Quadrant Three | Ministries | Empower |
| Quadrant Four | Outreach | Engage |

## Diagram 5A

Some leave this intense personalizing to a later time, perhaps during the process of transformation or revitalization. Some do this work up front. Settling on words to indicate the mission of the church brings health and alignment. It does not result in movement but aligns the church toward mission; it makes movement possible.

**Strategize: Formulate a health plan for the body.**

The Church Life Model is a healthy church model, but the road to health and vitality will need a strategy. Individual churches must sort through the options and formulate a strategic plan that fits their particular congregation. Church Life offers two catalysts that can generate movement toward strength—assessment and a health plan.

> This personalizing yields into a new, soft entity with formable components ready for growth and movement.

One of the vital elements available to the local assembly is assessment. Honest evaluation and in-depth appraisal can provide good information for those leaders who choose to take on the task of formulating a health plan. The Church Life Function Assessment provides a comprehensive, subjective evaluation of the church for each of the fifteen systems of the model. An in-depth discussion of this assessment occurs in the latter portion of this chapter.

Another group of evaluative tools provided by Church Life includes obstacle and solution assessments for each of the quadrants and the two segments of the core. These sixty-item assessments furnish evaluative statements for each of the functions located in the missional quadrants and core, as well as checklists naming the obstacles and solutions inherent in these areas. Leaders who choose to use these tools can identify the strengths and weaknesses of the systems. Also, the checklists of obstacles and solutions give assessors an opportunity to identify those missing and weak parts for each quadrant.

A second catalyst for strategizing is developing a written health plan. Church Life provides an introductory list of possible action items for the health plan. Some of these items appear in the following list:

1. Identify and celebrate healthy functioning where applicable. Celebration and commendation for those parts that show optimal vitality sows hope and encouragement within the whole church.
2. Identify ways to strengthen those systems that have healthy parts. Upon assessment, if a particular system shows heartiness, then observe all the parts within this system. Identify those individual pieces that could use some bolstering, and write these into the health plan as parts to firm up.
3. Note pieces that are missing. Write into the health plan some projected initiatory steps to supply the missing necessary elements of that function. Include anticipated dates for beginning these steps.
4. Identify any dysfunctional systems. Admit the degree of dysfunction and estimate the recovery time needed to restore vitality to these areas. Project a date for the work to begin in the dysfunctional systems.

5. Determine those items on the health plan that qualify for a quick fix or that will produce immediate results. Place these first on the health plan list. Then, note those items that will take more time investment; position these farther down on the list.

The key words *memorize, visualize, personalize,* and *strategize* serve well to indicate those central behaviors that form the global patterns of engagement for the Church Life Model. Utilize these words with their corresponding behaviors to set direction toward amalgamating an existing church with the paradigm and principles. Our attention will now focus on two specific patterns of engagement.

## Specific Patterns of Engagement

Pastors attending Church Life cohorts usually ask the same question at the end of the first session: Where do I begin? Spiritual health and movement begin with prayer and prophetic proclamation. God's life, God's heart, God's mission must create a flow into the church and then through the church to the community. So the initial, specific behaviors of engagement begin in prayer and preaching.

**Initiations in prayer**

The first initiative in prayer involves encouraging congregrants in the practice of personal devotion, relationship time with God. If the first movement of spiritual formation initiates by connecting with God, then advocating personal relationship with God on a regular basis will spur the church to fresh connectivity. These connections serve as sparks of renewed spiritual life within the body. Most church leaders we have queried believe that less than 25 percent of American Christians observe a regular conversation (prayer time) with God. Church Life advocates a regular emphasis on personal, private devotions along with good suggestions about how to build and deepen

> This connection, this breathing of the presence, this resuscitation of the church body cannot be underestimated.

one's relationship with God. This encouragement can never evolve into a legal commitment or a duty; it must remain a love commitment to Christ based upon the words of Matthew 22:37: "Love the Lord your God with all your heart and with all your soul and with all your mind."

Second, consider initiating new behaviors of corporate prayer. In American churches, corporate prayer has waned as a means of grace to connect the leaders of the church with God. The pastor prays for the people, and prayer for personal needs still resounds through the halls of the church, but corporate prayer by the people of God will bring new streams of health and vitality to the congregation. (See Psalm 66:19; Isaiah 40:9; Zechariah 8:20–22; and Acts 4:24–31.)

Praying with scriptural prayer models supplies a necessary mode of operation for corporate prayer. They serve to move pray-ers along in orderly ways in their praises and requests.

The focus of this prayer aims toward God's agenda and His mission for the people of this church at this time in this context. Most of the spiritual movements and awakenings recorded in church history initiated when people gathered for corporate prayer. This connection, this breathing of the presence, this resuscitation of the church body cannot be underestimated. This corporate prayer for the advancement of God's kingdom was encouraged greatly by men like Jonathan Edwards[1] during the early years of American history. We experienced the practice of corporate prayer on a mega-scale when we visited the Yoido Full Gospel Church in Seoul, Korea, in the fall of 1984. This was the first time we saw several thousand pray-ers join in united prayer for the advancement of God's mission.

Praying with scriptural prayer models supplies a necessary mode of operation for corporate prayer. They serve to move pray-ers along in orderly ways in their praises and requests. These models form their content by observing the present activity of God and then overlaying this activity with those Scriptures that record similar occurrences. From the selected Scripture, the prayer model gleans the revelation given about God and the request that comes as a response. For example, if Psalm 23 (KJV) declares that "the LORD is my shepherd; I shall not want," then the revelation emerges from the text that our Lord cares for us just as a shepherd cares for the sheep, providing for all their needs. We then request that He shepherd us and supply all of our needs. (A sample prayer model appears in Appendix A.)

**Initiations in preaching**

Both prayer and proclamation set the atmosphere of any church. In most Spirit-filled congregations, *preaching* means "prophetic proclamation." Also in these environs, the work of preaching declares the Word, ways, and will of God in the contemporary setting. Pastors can grasp these opportunities to declare to their constituents the divine urgencies that spring from engagement with the model and initiations in prayer. Preaching from the Old Testament exilic periods assists members in identifying the movements needed to align with the mission of God for the church today.

Choosing appropriate biblical metaphors helps church leaders connect with the streams of thought about the church and its purposes in this generation. The Old Testament books of the major prophets and minor prophets are rich with metaphors, prophetic words, and divine urgencies, as are the New Testament books of Hebrews and Revelation. Health, mission, spirituality, community, discipleship, outreach—all of these are divine urgencies for the contemporary church.

Excellent prophetic preaching occurs at the convergence point of divine urgencies and universal human needs. If the pastor can find fresh wells of living water provided by God for the present season of the church, the preparing, packaging, and delivering of these insights will provide good spiritual nourishment for the congregation. If the pastor can also discern the universal human need God longs to meet, then the miracle of deep soul satisfaction occurs within the listeners. This is prophetic preaching at its best. Often this convergence occurs in seasons. Sermon series preached from this convergence point between divine spiritual wells and real human need bring renewal and growth for the constituents.

Both the global and specific patterns of engagement discussed in this section give pastors and leaders suggestions for beginning work with the Church Life Model. They provide avenues for initiation in the first phases of utilization. To accompany the model, Church Life also suggests a transformation process that offers multiple ideas for advancement methodologies. These concepts, as stated previously, will provide the content for a subsequent publication. Our discussion will now move to an overview of the statistical information reported from the many churches and leaders who have engaged the model and participated in the Church Life Function Assessment.

## The Church Life Function Assessment

Like the model, the Church Life Function Assessment has evolved over the years. Its formation began early in the process and coincided with the development of the model. Repeated use of the assessment within pastoral and educational cohorts, along with openness to feedback from participants, have brought clarity to the one hundred and fifty statements formulated to evaluate the activity and work of the fifteen vital functions or systems within the church.

As with any subjective assessment, the statements offered for evaluation keys to a defined baseline of content. For instance, the Myers-Briggs Type Indicator, a well-known personality assessment, evaluates a person's preferences, tendencies, and characteristics on four defined scales with clearly defined meanings. Likewise, the fifteen functions defined in chapter 4 of this text furnish the specific processes evaluated in this assessment. Each of the fifteen functions receives assessment using ten items evaluated on a ten-point scale. On that scale, one equals poor, five equals average, and ten equals excellent.

It is believed that assessment credibility increases by compiling multiple assessments from church leaders, pastors, staff, and lay leadership. In the fall of 2004, software was developed for Church Life that does the work of recording an individual's responses in a database and then producing reports that synthesize responses into meaningful statements. Pastors receive only the composite report that results from the input of several individual responses.

In May 2010 a reliability analysis was performed for the Church Life Function Assessment. Responses from seventy-seven assessments furnished the data used to identify reliability of the instrument with regard to internal consistency. The following paragraph summarizes those findings.

> This analysis suggests the items for each of the subscales are of sufficient quality to demonstrate good internal consistency as each of the subscales have a Cronbach's alpha greater than α=.700 and all but one have Cronbach's alpha greater than α=.800. Suggestions are made for improving eight of the subscales, but they are not required. It would likely be more advantageous to look at the wording of the identified items to see how they could be improved rather than removing them from the instrument.[2]

Validity studies have not occurred formally, but the last item of the Church Life Model Survey asked participants (eighty-seven pastors) to rate the validity of the results of the assessment(s) for their local churches. All participants believed the assessment gave valid results for their congregations, with seventy-nine respondents (91 percent) stating that the validity was either good (thirty respondents) or excellent (forty-nine respondents). From these responses, it appears that those who participated in the survey have confidence in the assessment and have found the results reported by the assessment to be valid.

For the purposes of this publication, we asked for a composite report of all the assessments in one of our Church Life Function Assessment databases. Seeing the combined responses of more than six thousand individual member assessments from over eleven hundred churches reveals interesting data about Spirit-filled churches in America. Some of the information from this composite report appears in Diagram 5B.

## Church Life Function Assessment

| | |
|---|---|
| (1) Leadership | 83% |
| (2) Vision/Mission | 70% |
| (3) Spiritual Life | 74% |
| (4) Preaching/Teaching | 83% |
| (5) Worship | 78% |
| (6) Assimilation | 66% |
| (7) Care/Fellowship | 70% |
| (8) Small Groups | 64% |
| (9) Ministries | 64% |
| (10) Discipleship | 65% |
| (11) Evangelism/Missions | 64% |
| (12) Public Relations | 68% |
| (13) Decision-Making | 70% |
| (14) Finances | 71% |
| (15) Facilities | 71% |

Assessment for:

All Churches with
Any Church Affiliation
and Attendance

Assessor:

Overall Composite

Top 3 Functions

(4) Preaching/Teaching 83%
(1) Leadership 83%
(5) Worship 78%

Lowest 3 Functions

(8) Small Groups 64%
(9) Ministries 64%
(11) Evangelism/Missions 64%

**Diagram 5B**

Seeing these components of the assessment report with their multiple indicators accentuates the comprehensive nature of the Church Life Model and this assessment. This view helps one to observe the fifteen vital functions that release energy or create drain upon the church and the relative strength each provides. The report gives a comparison of the strengths of each of the missional quadrants.

Church Life promotes the idea that a function or quadrant becomes more attractive and gives impetus to the entire system when evaluated near the 80 percent point. An airplane can reach one hundred and thirty miles and hour, but if lift for that aircraft occurs at one hundred and thirty-five, the plane will not rise until it reaches that point. We have observed that something like lift occurs at the 80 percent mark; all six quadrants need to reach 80 percent health for the church to operate in strength and move forward. Health in one area cannot compensate for a lack of health in another. If the care system is broken, more prayer in the spiritual life system will not take care of the dysfunction in spiritual community.

Health in one area cannot compensate for a lack of health in another. If the care system is broken, more prayer in the spiritual life system will not take care of the dysfunction in spiritual community.

What is the good news for any church that decides to engage the Church Life Model? The good news is the belief that most dysfunction and missing pieces can receive correction and restoration. For most churches, it takes about two years to make the necessary adjustments so the church can begin functioning well. All quadrants must receive attention simultaneously. A vehicle must have all four wheels functioning well for the car to move forward; otherwise, it could continue to circle with minimal movement but no forward progress.

Note that the spiritual life quadrant boasts the highest evaluation—78 percent. All other missional quadrants are in the mid-60-percent range. This convinces the observer that while these churches show reasonable spiritual health, their relational, ministry, and outreach quadrants need attention. It is interesting that the quadrant where most of the staff members of churches concentrate their efforts may not produce as much health as one may assume. The management role in the bottom of the core, while above the 70 percent mark, shows some drag on the leadership strength of the church.

Note the strongest functions are those that directly interface with the pastor—preaching/teaching, leadership, and worship. The areas of small groups, ministries, and evangelism carry the lowest evaluations (64 percent). This could indicate a lack of sufficient leadership training and member involvement in these vital areas of the body. A "healthiest to least healthy" listing of the functions appears in Diagram 5C.

**Healthiest to Least Healthy Functions**

| | |
|---|---|
| Preaching/Teaching | 83% |
| Leadership | 83% |
| Worship | 78% |
| Spiritual Life | 74% |
| Facilities | 71% |
| Finances | 71% |
| Decision-Making | 70% |
| Care/Fellowship | 70% |
| Vision/Mission | 70% |
| Public Relations | 68% |
| Assimilation | 66% |
| Discipleship | 65% |
| Small Groups | 64% |
| Ministries | 64% |
| Evangelism/Missions | 64% |

**Diagram 5C**

This chapter provided engagement patterns for pastors desiring to utilize the Church Life Model in an existing church. Global and specific patterns gave suggested behaviors and initiatory activities. One of the suggestions for engagement highlighted using the Church Life Function Assessment. A discussion of the assessment and the value of its use gave readers a chance to become somewhat acquainted with this tool. This chapter also provided a brief review of selected components from a composite assessment from the Church Life Assessment database involving a large number of churches and leaders. The discussion pointed to some very interesting observations drawn from this composite report.

# 6

# WHAT DID THE CHURCH LIFE MODEL SURVEY REVEAL?

*Without counsel, plans go awry, but in the multitude of counselors they are established.*

—Proverbs 15:22, NKJV

THE CHURCH LIFE Model did not evolve as simply a good idea for the organization of the spiritual organism called the church. As stated, the goal of the work centered upon finding ways for leaders to master the complexity of the tasks assigned to them both by biblical mandate and by the words of the Master. This framework evolved over time as groups of pastors processed its various components and as we kneaded together, with prayer and meditation, the many insights and discernments that resulted from these intensely valuable collaboration moments.

As the model stabilized in format, we began to utilize it in various settings to test its validity and credibility. Over the past six years, the model has gained momentum among pastors in the United States as Church Life has conducted pastoral cohorts in more than fifteen states.

In addition, the model has gained recognition in various educational environments. Much discussion has resulted as pastors and leaders have engaged the model in their ministry contexts. The feedback received from these venues has proven valuable in adjusting various principles and concepts surrounding the model.

In February 2011, as we approached the deadline for this publication, we asked some of the constituents who have utilized the model in their congregations in the United States to participate in a Church Life Model survey. This survey provided participants the opportunity to furnish concrete data about their ministry tenures, their engagement with the model, their opinions concerning its usefulness and effectiveness, and their recommendations of its viability for use by other pastors. Eighty-seven leaders, mostly senior pastors, from various churches responded to the survey. Some of these leaders have received in-depth training in the church life principles and process. All of these churches would describe themselves as Spirit-filled, Pentecostal, or Charismatic. This chapter provides the results of this survey and some discussion and analysis of the responses. (A copy of the survey appears in Diagram 6A.)

## Church Life Model Survey

**1. How long have you pastored your present church?**

- Less than 3 years
- 3 to 5 years
- 5 to 10 years
- 10 to 20 years
- Over 20 years

**2. What percentage of the Church Life Model and principles have you implemented in your church?**

- None
- Less than 20%
- 20 to 39%
- 40 to 59%
- 60 to 79%
- 80% or greater

**3. How long have you utilized the Church Life Model and principles?**

- Less than one year
- One to two years
- Two to five years
- Five to eight years
- More than eight years
- None

**4. How do you rate your understanding of the Church Life Model?**

- Do Not Understand
- Understand Somewhat
- Average Understanding
- Understand Well
- Understand Very Well

**5. Indicate the value of the Church Life Model for the church in the following areas?**

| | No Value | Some Value | Average Value | Good Value | Excellent Value |
|---|---|---|---|---|---|
| **Missional Model** | ○ | ○ | ○ | ○ | ○ |
| **Universal Model** | ○ | ○ | ○ | ○ | ○ |
| **Comprehensive Model** | ○ | ○ | ○ | ○ | ○ |
| **Pentecostal Model** | ○ | ○ | ○ | ○ | ○ |
| **Developmental Model** | ○ | ○ | ○ | ○ | ○ |
| **Systemic Model** | ○ | ○ | ○ | ○ | ○ |
| **Visual Model** | ○ | ○ | ○ | ○ | ○ |
| **Structural Model** | ○ | ○ | ○ | ○ | ○ |
| **Apostolic Model** | ○ | ○ | ○ | ○ | ○ |
| **Unifying Model** | ○ | ○ | ○ | ○ | ○ |

**6. Choose the Church Life vital functions one through seven (1-7) that you have strengthened in the church and rate the measure of health benefit received.**

| | No Health Benefit | Some Health Benefit | Average Health Benefit | Good Health Benefit | Excellent Health Benefit |
|---|---|---|---|---|---|
| **Leadership** | ○ | ○ | ○ | ○ | ○ |
| **Vision/Mission** | ○ | ○ | ○ | ○ | ○ |
| **Spiritual Life** | ○ | ○ | ○ | ○ | ○ |
| **Preaching/Teaching** | ○ | ○ | ○ | ○ | ○ |
| **Worship** | ○ | ○ | ○ | ○ | ○ |
| **Assimilation** | ○ | ○ | ○ | ○ | ○ |
| **Care/Fellowship** | ○ | ○ | ○ | ○ | ○ |

**7. Choose the Church Life vital functions eight through fifteen (8-15) that you have strengthened in the church and rate the measure of health benefit received.**

| | No Health Benefit | Some Health Benefit | Average Health Benefit | Good Health Benefit | Excellent Health Benefit |
|---|---|---|---|---|---|
| **Small Groups** | ○ | ○ | ○ | ○ | ○ |
| **Ministries** | ○ | ○ | ○ | ○ | ○ |
| **Discipleship** | ○ | ○ | ○ | ○ | ○ |
| **Outreach** [Evangelism/Missions] | ○ | ○ | ○ | ○ | ○ |
| **Public Relations** | ○ | ○ | ○ | ○ | ○ |
| **Decision Making** | ○ | ○ | ○ | ○ | ○ |
| **Finances** | ○ | ○ | ○ | ○ | ○ |
| **Facilities** | ○ | ○ | ○ | ○ | ○ |

**8. Give an overall rating of increased internal health that has resulted since engaging the Church Life Model.**

- None
- Between 1% and 19%
- Between 20% and 39%
- Between 40% and 59%
- Between 60% and 79%
- 80% or greater

**9. Choose from the following list those items that describe your personal leadership since receiving training in the Church Life Model.**

- Renewed Hope
- Increased Confidence
- More Competent Leader
- Increased Understanding of the Church
- Spiritually Renewed
- More Prayerful
- More Discerning of the Activity of Christ
- More Empowering of Others
- More Capable Team Facilitator
- Better Strategic Planner

**10. What increase in Sunday attendance has the church experienced since engaging the Church Life Model?**

- None
- 1% to 19%
- 20% to 39%
- 40% to 59%
- 60% to 79%
- 80% and More

**11. What best describes the recommendation you would give the Church Life Model as a valid model for churches?**

- Would not recommend
- Would recommend with caution
- Would recommend
- Would recommend highly

**12. If you assessed the church using the Church Life Function Assessment, how would you rate the validity of the results of the assessment?**

- Did not assess the church
- Not valid at all
- Somewhat valid
- Average validity
- Good validity
- Excellent validity

## DIAGRAM 6A

Each question of the survey asked for information pertinent to the participants' use of the model in their church contexts. Some items focused on the respondents' personal, subjective evaluations of its value and effectiveness, and others asked for more concrete, quantitative data. This informational and opinion survey provided significant feedback of each pastor's engagement of the model and his or her perceived benefit resulting from its use within the church. The last survey item asked for an evaluation of the validity of the Church Life Function Assessment. The composite results from each item of the survey appear in the following pages with comments and discussion.

Item one (Diagram 6B) simply gives an idea of the tenure of the pastors responding to the survey. Only 16 percent have served five years or less in the churches where they engaged the Church Life Model. Forty-seven percent have led their congregations for ten years or more with nineteen pastors (21.8 percent) serving twenty or more years in their present locations. The largest single category of respondents, 35.6 percent, has led their present churches from five to ten years. Conclusions drawn from the survey participants indicate that 82.6 percent have stayed more than five years at the churches where they have engaged the Church Life Model, and almost half (47 percent) have a tenure of ten years or more.

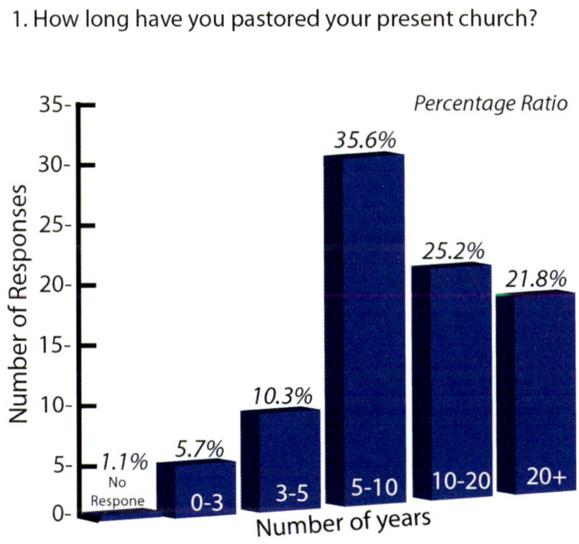


**DIAGRAM 6B**

Items two and three (Diagrams 6C and 6D) asked for information regarding the implementation of the model and its principles and the length of time that the congregation has engaged the model. Sixty-four respondents (73.4 percent) had implemented 40 percent or more of the concepts at the time of the survey, with twenty-one of these pastors (24.1 percent) saying they have reached an implementation stage of 80 percent or greater. Only eight pastors have implemented less than 20 percent. As to the length of time of implementation, fifty-three leaders (61.5 percent) have utilized the model more than two years, with nearly 13 percent having engaged the model five years or more. Thirteen respondents are still in their first year of implementation. Conclusions drawn from the results of these items indicate that most of the survey participants are engaged in implementing the model in their local ministry environs, and most of them have progressed past the first year of implementation.

2. What percentage of the Church Life Model and principles have you implemented in your church?

3. How long have you utilized the Church Life Model and principles?

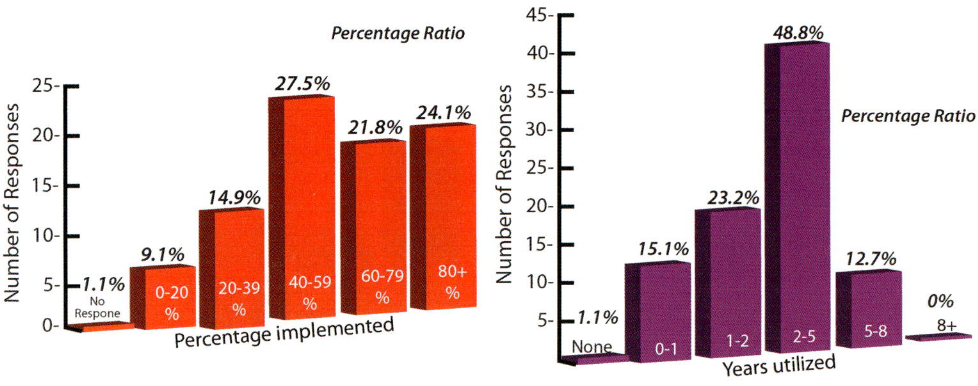


## DIAGRAMS 6C AND 6D

Participants rated their understanding of the Church Life Model in item four (Diagram 6E). Forty-five respondents said they understand the model "well," with another twenty-four believing they understand it "very well." These combined totals reflect that 80 percent of those surveyed indicate an above average understanding of the model. Only three pastors expressed that they understood the model "somewhat," with thirteen owning an "average" understanding.

A good summary statement from this item comes from the rating score. The rating score results from adding all the responses of all the respondents using the numerals 1 through 5 and then dividing the sum of the responses by the total number of participants. When rounded, the rating score for item four is 4.1. This indicates that most of the respondents say that they "understand well" the concepts of the Church Life Model.

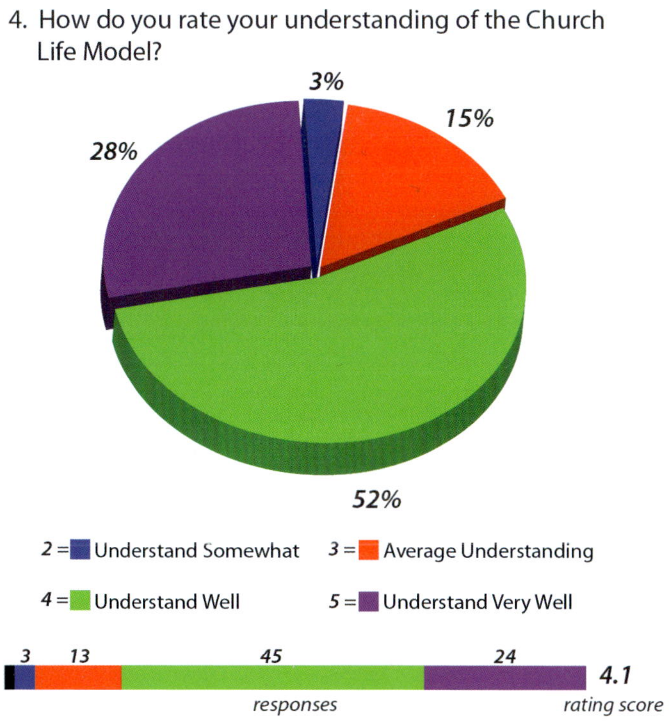


## Diagram 6E

The next survey item, item five (Diagram 6F), asked participants to indicate their perceived values of the model for their congregations. Utilizing the ten values discussed in chapter 3, this survey item asked respondents to rate these values on a scale of 1 through 5, from "no value" to "excellent value." Those surveyed expressed that their congregations value the model most highly because it is missional (4.6), because it is Spirit-filled or Pentecostal (4.6), and because it is systemic (4.6).

On another level of detail for this item of the survey, sixty pastors (71 percent) gave the systemic value of the model a score of 5, indicating that the systems approach offered by the model has excellent value for the congregation. None of the ten values fell below a rating of 4.3. The results of the responses to this item indicate that most perceived each of the values of the Church Life Model discussed in chapter 3 offers "good value" or "excellent value" to congregations that have engaged the model.

Those surveyed expressed that their congregations value the model most highly because it is missional (4.6), because it is Spirit-filled or Pentecostal (4.6), and because it is systemic (4.6).

An important additional comment on the results of item five includes emphasizing, as previously stated, that those pastors and churches participating in this survey would describe themselves as Pentecostal, Spirit-filled, or Charismatic congregations. They value a model that provides openness to the presence of the Trinity in their congregational meetings and provides encouragement for members to exercise their spiritual gifts. On this point, we would draw attention to the overwhelming survey bias of the participants.

5. Indicate the value of the Church Life Model for the church in the following areas.

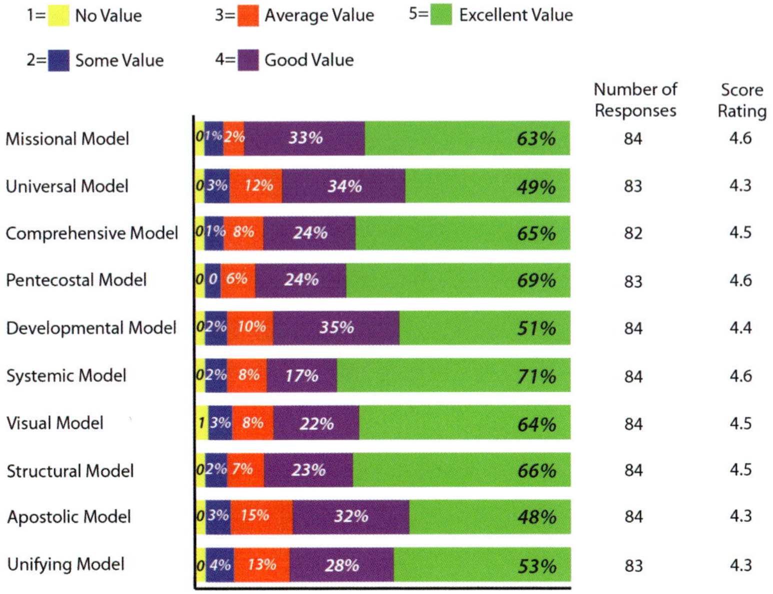


## Diagram 6F

Items six and seven (Diagrams 6G and 6H) asked those who took part in the survey to identify those functions of the model (the fifteen vital functions described in chapter 4) that they worked to strengthen in the church. After identifying the strengthened function, respondents then rated the perceived health benefit received by the church as a result of this action. The systems of leadership and vision/mission received the highest rating scores. Leadership received a rating score of 4.5, with 53 percent reporting an "excellent health benefit" for the church when this function was strengthened. Vision/mission came in a very close second with a 4.4 rating score and 48 percent declaring this function as an "excellent health benefit."

Other very highly rated functions included spiritual life, assimilation, care/fellowship, preaching/teaching, discipleship, decision-making, worship, and public relations. Respondents assigned a rating of 5 the least number of times to the functions of finances and facilities. These received the lowest rating scores, 3.8 and 3.7 respectively.

Overall conclusions drawn from the health benefit rating of the fifteen vital functions indicate high "average" to "excellent health benefit" for all functions. Another specific comment about this item points to the fact that pastors perceived as highest the two functions that they must personally strengthen during the initial stages of engagement with the model. Because they pour much personal energy, initiation, and involvement into the health of leadership and vision/mission, pastors may be more sensitive to the benefit derived from strengthening these functions. They may have experienced more results from these functions early in the engagement process. Their leaders and members of the congregation may have given much immediate positive feedback on these two functions of the leadership core.

Overall conclusions drawn from the health benefit rating of the fifteen vital functions indicate high "average" to "excellent health benefit" for all functions.

6. Choose the Church Life vital functions one through seven (1-7) that you have strengthened in the church and rate the measure of health benefit received.

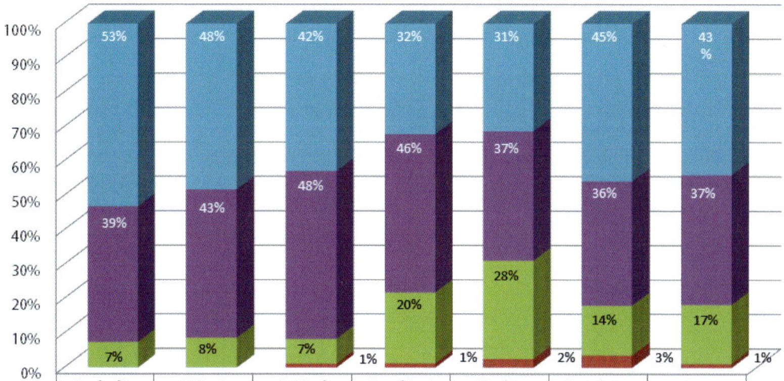


| | Leadership | Vision / Mission | Spiritual Life | Preaching / Teaching | Worship | Assimilation | Care / Fellowship |
|---|---|---|---|---|---|---|---|
| Excellent Health Benefit | 43 | 39 | 36 | 25 | 24 | 38 | 36 |
| Good Health Benefit | 32 | 35 | 41 | 36 | 29 | 30 | 31 |
| Average Health Benefit | 6 | 7 | 6 | 16 | 22 | 12 | 14 |
| Some Health Benefit | 0 | 0 | 1 | 1 | 2 | 3 | 1 |
| No Health Benefit | 0 | 0 | 0 | 0 | 0 | 0 | 0 |
| **Rating Score** | 4.5 | 4.4 | 4.3 | 4.1 | 4.0 | 4.2 | 4.2 |

Number of Responses

7. Choose the Church Life vital functions eight through fifteen (8-15) that you have strengthened in the church and rate the measure of health benefit received.

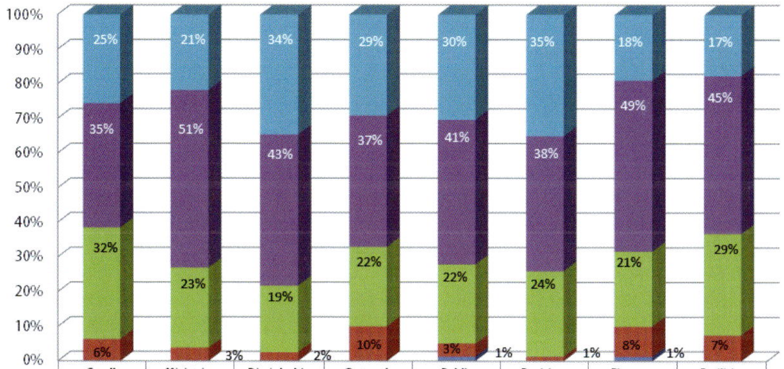


| | Small Groups | Ministries | Discipleship | Outreach | Public Relations | Decision-Making | Finances | Facilities |
|---|---|---|---|---|---|---|---|---|
| Excellent Health Benefit | 20 | 17 | 27 | 23 | 24 | 27 | 15 | 14 |
| Good Health Benefit | 28 | 40 | 34 | 30 | 33 | 30 | 39 | 36 |
| Average Health Benefit | 25 | 18 | 15 | 18 | 18 | 19 | 17 | 23 |
| Some Health Benefit | 5 | 3 | 2 | 8 | 3 | 1 | 7 | 6 |
| No Health Benefit | 0 | 0 | 0 | 0 | 1 | 0 | 1 | 0 |
| **Rating Score** | 3.8 | 3.9 | 4.1 | 3.9 | 4.0 | 4.1 | 3.8 | 3.7 |

Number of Responses

## Diagrams 6G and 6H

Moving on to item eight (Diagram 6I), pastors then gave an overall rating of increased internal health resulting from engagement with the Church Life Model. This item asked for a very subjective quantification. Only nine respondents (10.3 percent) perceived a health increase of 19 percent or lower. Sixteen indicated that their congregations received an increase of 80 percent or greater in internal health. The majority of the respondents (forty-eight) perceived between 40 percent and 79 percent increase in internal health of the church. The results of these responses indicate a strong internal movement toward health and vitality in churches that engage the model. However, the noteworthy observation for this item involves making sure that the pastors' perceptions of movement toward internal health align with other health indicators within the congregation.

The results of these responses indicate a strong internal movement toward health and vitality in churches that engage the model.

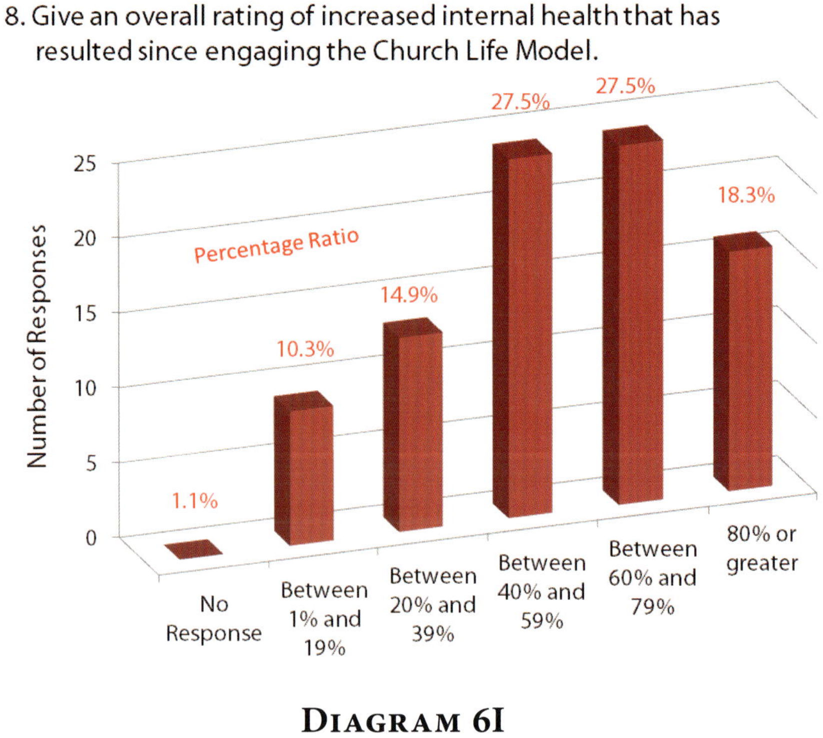


DIAGRAM 6I

Item nine (Diagram 6J) asked pastors to choose from a given list of descriptors that they believe describe their leadership since receiving training in the Church Life Model. Participants could choose any or all of the choices provided. Those descriptors chosen the most times included "increased understanding of the church" (eighty), "more competent leader" (seventy-seven), and "better strategic planner" (sixty-nine). "Increased confidence" (sixty-six) and "more empowering of others" (sixty-two) were next in order of preference.

We received great encouragement from responses to item nine of the survey. First indicators from this initial survey appear to suggest that training in the Church Life Model and its accompanying principles contribute significantly to the pastoral leader's ability to get his or her arms around the huge responsibility of leading the church. These responses align with the many verbal reports received from pastors in the Church Life cohort groups conducted over the past six years.

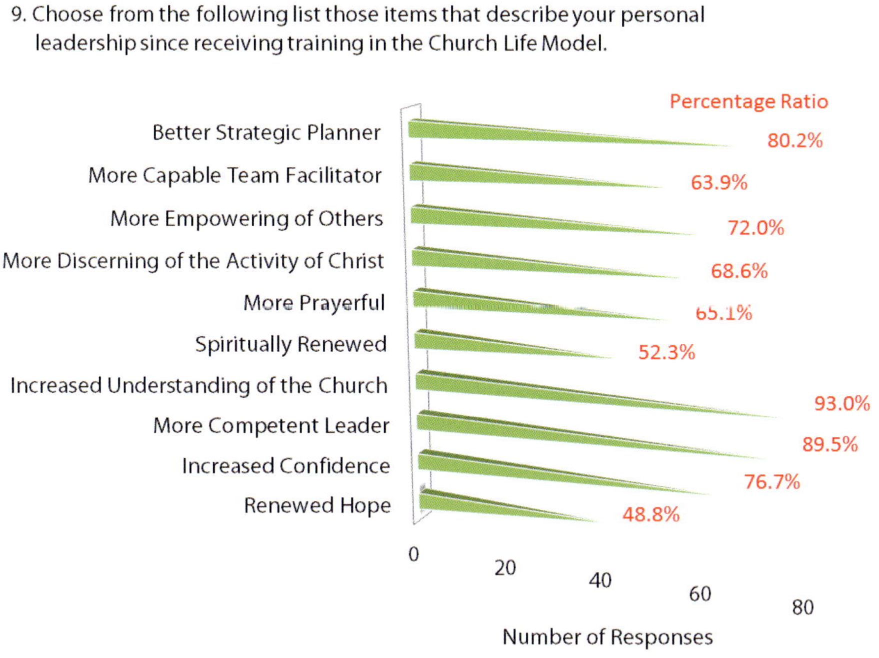


**DIAGRAM 6J**

Responses for item ten (Diagram 6K) of the survey provide a bit more concrete qualitative data. This item asked pastors to indicate increases in Sunday attendance since engaging the Church Life Model. Eight respondents (9.1 percent) reported no increase in attendance. On the opposite side of the spectrum, three pastors (3.4 percent) indicated increases of 80 percent or more. Most pastors (seventy-two respondents) indicated an increase from 1 percent to 60 percent in the Sunday morning attendance of the church. Conclusions from this survey item indicate that most of the time the congregation experiences a participation increase when leaders engage the Church Life Model.

10. What increase in Sunday attendance has the church experienced since engaging the Church Life Model?

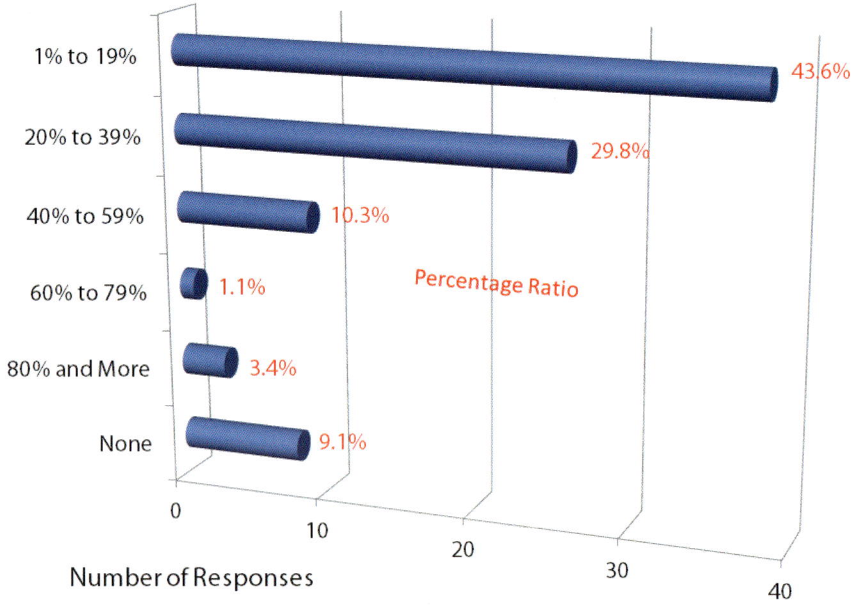


**DIAGRAM 6K**

Participants are asked in item eleven (Diagram 6L) about their recommendations of the Church Life Model as a valid model for churches to utilize. All respondents recommended the model to their peers. Seventy-seven participants (88.5 percent) indicated that they would "recommend highly" the model, eight (9.1 percent) would "recommend," and one respondent would "recommend with caution." A conclusion from this survey item indicates that most pastors who have engaged the model and participated in this survey express confidence in the model's usefulness, so much so that they would recommend it to other pastors and leaders.

All respondents recommended the model to their peers.

11. What best describes the recommendation you would give the Church Life Model as a valid model for churches?

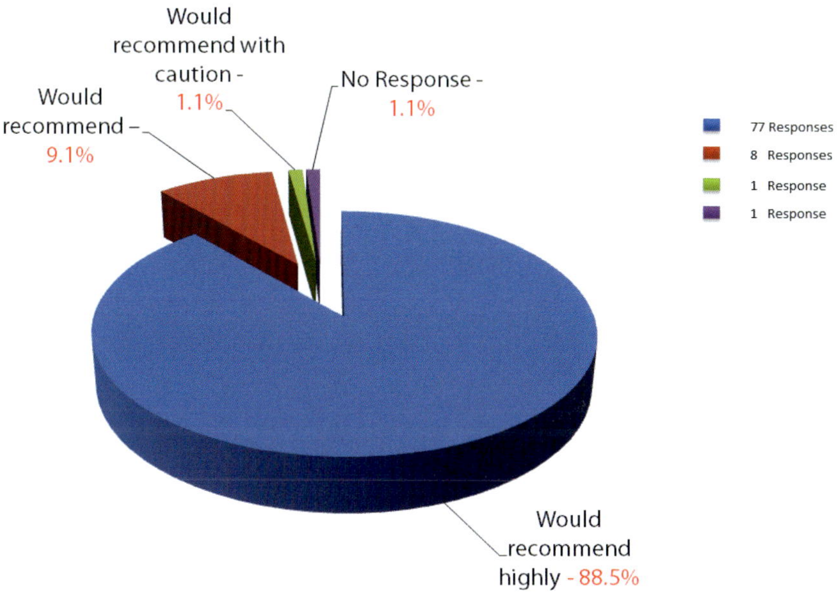


## Diagram 6L

The last survey item, item twelve (Diagram 6M), gave participants the opportunity to state their subjective evaluation of the validity of the Church Life Function Assessment. Two of the participants had not utilized the assessment at the time of the survey. Seventy-nine participants (90.7 percent) indicated an evaluation of either "good validity" or "excellent validity." Five reported an evaluation of "somewhat valid" or "average validity." A conclusion gained from this item indicates that the Church Life Function Assessment has proven a valid tool of assessment for most of the pastors participating in this survey.

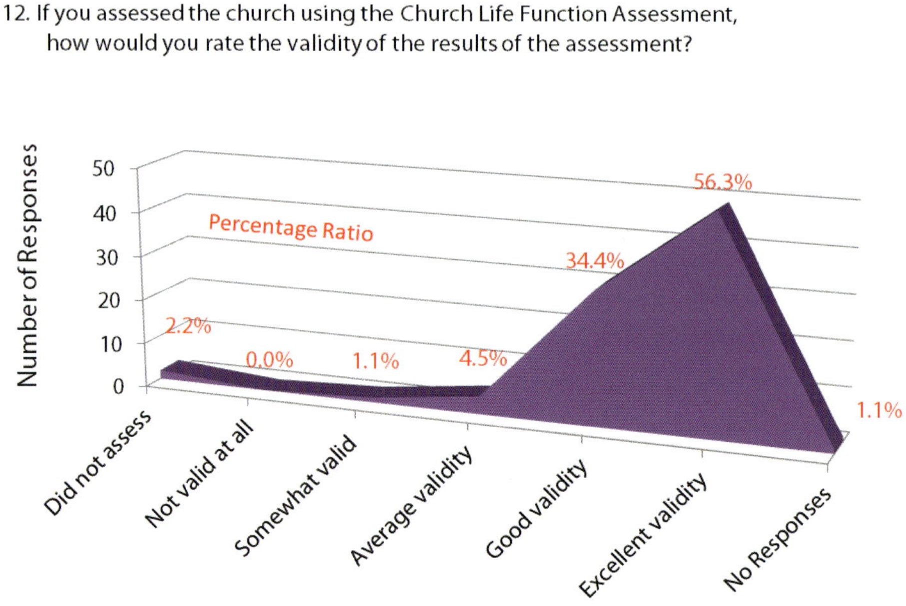


**DIAGRAM 6M**

In this chapter, we have shared the results of a Church Life Model Survey conducted in February 2011, immediately before publication of this work. Discussion of the responses has helped to produce some broad conclusions. A listing of these conclusions appears on the following page.

## Conclusions Drawn from the Church Life Model Survey

1. Participants have average to long tenure at their churches.
2. Respondents have implemented 40 percent or more of the model principles and concepts, and most have utilized the model for more than a year.
3. Most understand well the concepts of the Church Life Model.
4. Respondents reported that the model offers good and excellent value to their congregations.
5. Participants find the fifteen vital functions provide high health benefit for their churches.
6. Strong internal movement toward health and vitality occurs in churches that engage the model.
7. Training in the Church Life Model concepts contributes significantly to the pastoral leader's perceived leadership abilities.
8. Most of the time congregations experience a participation increase on Sunday mornings when they engage the Church Life Model.
9. Participants in the survey highly recommended utilization of the model by other churches. The Church Life Function Assessment proved a valid tool of assessment for the respondents.

# 7

# WHAT COMES NEXT?

*I will stand my watch and set myself on the rampart, and watch to see what He will say to me.*

—Habakkuk 2:1, NKJV

IN THE BEGINNING chapter, we alerted readers to the reasons for writing about the Church Life Model, its formation, design, value, and usefulness. Those purposes, simply stated, include the following: to fulfill God's purpose, to advance personal mission, to respond to counsel, to give broader access, to encourage pastors, and to edify the church. Here at the conclusion of this first publication task, attention focuses on what comes next.

We function within the privileges and responsibilities that come with sharing and refining the principles and concepts of Church Life. Often the assignments feel overwhelming, as was the case with this publication. The pathway, however, becomes clearer and more doable as we progress from obedience to obedience. Writing to make the ideas plain and usable has proven much more difficult than we first assumed. The projections for additional publications that follow do not serve as commitments but only our best assertions within the grand scheme of God's will.

Next on the horizon for publication includes a work that will contain the spiritual life components of Church Life. This book will provide in-depth explanations of spiritual concepts like passionate congregational prayer, contemplative prayer, layered spirituality, personal devotion, practice of disciplines, and prayer models. Prayer resources from the many pastors and leaders involved in Church Life pastoral cohorts will make this publication a most useful compilation of those spiritual life components that are presently bringing health and renewal throughout the United States and other nations of the world. This manuscript will result from collaboration with pastors of healthy churches that pulsate with the dynamic presence of Christ.

Another subsequent publication will address the need for church transformation and revitalization. The world changes constantly; the church struggles to adapt. Often it finds its methods and points of relevance dulled by the shifting currents of change. This text will address some of the major causes for lack of health and decline in Spirit-filled churches in America. Some of these issues include irrelevance, culture barriers, lack of spiritual vitality, and relational difficulties. This work will integrate a theology of transformation with a good, practical process for making needed changes in existing churches. It will identify the transformational process the church can initiate to accommodate the paradigmatic changes necessary for health and vitality. The present condition of the church, including its strengths and weaknesses will be identified. Then, the process to change any church will occupy the major portion of the book. The theology of revitalization and a transformational process included in this work will enhance its core message and usefulness for contemporary churches.

Church Life also recognizes the need for a comprehensive investigation of the fifteen vital functions summarized in chapter 4. We intend to publish a work that devotes a chapter to each function or system, giving a comprehensive definition and description of each. Devoting a chapter to each will also provide the opportunity to explain all of the major components of the system and how they could potentially work in the local church environment.

Completing this initial publication, *The Church Life Model: A Biblical Schema for the Spirit-filled Church*, provides pastors and leaders with a well-developed foundation of thought that warrants much future investigation, dialogue, and discovery. We welcome your comments and further investigation into the resources of Church Life. You will find us on the Web at churchliferesources.org.

# APPENDIX A

# A SAMPLE VERSION OF THE CHURCH LIFE FUNCTION ASSESSMENT

THE COMPLETE VERSION of the Church Life Function Assessment, discussed in chapter 5, evaluates the health and vitality of the local church by indicating the strength and weakness of each of the fifteen vital functions or systems of the church. The fifteen vital functions summarized in chapter 4 are listed below.

- Leadership
- Vision/Mission
- Spiritual Life
- Preaching/Teaching
- Worship
- Assimilation
- Care/Fellowship
- Small Groups
- Ministries
- Discipleship

- Public Relations
- Evangelism/Missions
- Decision-Making
- Finances
- Facilities

In this sample version included as a preview of the complete assessment, evaluators respond to forty-five items centered on these fifteen functions. This short version of the assessment offers three evaluative statements for each of the functions listed. Each statement asks the assessor for an evaluation on a ten-point scale from 1 to 10. Adding the scores from each of the three statements applying to each function produces a total score based on a thirty-point-possible score for each system.

Comparing the total scores, highest and lowest, can give *some* indication of strength or weakness. While this version with only three statements for each function may provide some indication of the strength or weakness of each function, a full assessment can provide more reliable indications of health or lack of health for each of these areas.

Assessment credibility increases when all church leaders participate, including the senior pastor, staff, and lay leadership. Compiling appraisals from these three perspectives improves the scope and probability of a comprehensive and accurate evaluation. It is recommended that evaluators become familiar with the Church Life Model to fully understand the fifteen functions or systems and their vital roles in the process of church health.

Evaluate each statement thoughtfully and honestly, exercising care in using the full range of evaluation choices. Make evaluations on the basis of the present realities of the church, not the preferred or future realities. This assessment provides a "snapshot" of the church at this time. The assessor provides this picture from his or her perspective.

Respond to the following statements by selecting a number from 1 to 10. Write the number in the square provided at the end of each statement.

## EVALUATION RANGE

| 1 | 2 | 3 | 4 | 5 | 6 | 7 | 8 | 9 | 10 |
|---|---|---|---|---|---|---|---|---|---|
| Poor | | | | Average | | | | | Excellent |
| | | | | | | | | | |

1. The pastoral leaders exhibit exceptional leadership in the church. ______
2. The church's vision includes a balanced emphasis in the spiritual, relational, ministry, and evangelism areas. ______
3. The spiritual life of our church includes opportunities for participation in the spiritual disciplines, both privately and publicly. ______
4. The worship experience in our church services reveals God to the participants. ______
5. The preaching/teaching advances the congregation in their relationship with God. ______
6. We welcome visitors, new believers, and new members into our fellowship, and we work hard to connect them to the church body. ______
7. Every person in our church receives individualized and situational care. ______
8. In our congregation, we build spiritual community by connecting and networking existing relationships. ______
9. Our congregation has strong age-specific and gender-specific ministries. ______
10. The church has a simple, comprehensive plan of discipleship. ______

11. Our pastoral leaders have identified the unique receptive groups in the community, Christians and pre-Christians, that our church can reach. ______

12. Our church has a good reputation in the community. ______

13. The decision-makers of the church practice good problem-solving, conflict resolution, and risk-management principles and techniques. ______

14. Our church manages finances through a budgeting process. ______

15. An appropriate balance exists in the use of our church facilities between evangelism, worship, fellowship, education (discipleship), office space, parking, nursery, restrooms, and storage. ______

16. Our pastoral leaders exhibit godly character and self-leadership. ______

17. Our church leaders (pastoral and lay) investigated and discerned our unique vision/mission by listening to God, the church leadership, and the community. ______

18. A majority of the congregation participates regularly in the spiritual life activities of our church. ______

19. Our worship engages the participants at the point of their receptivity and needs. ______

20. The biblical truths presented in our church are communicated in culturally relevant language and style. ______

21. A comprehensive assimilation process exists in our church to welcome newcomers. ______

22. A strong sense of relational belonging (spiritual community) exists in our church. ______

23. Relational networks (small units) reach, keep, and mature believers in our church. ______

24. A motivated and adequate labor force of volunteers performs the ministries in our church. ______

25. Discipleship at our church develops a specific pathway of spiritual formation. ______

26. Our church provides structured pathways to connect and win pre-Christians. ______

27. The church uses a balance of internal media expressions (Web site, e-mail, Facebook, phone calls, personal contacts, print, video, etc.) to create congregational awareness of our mission and ministries. ______

28. The overall organizational structure of the church aligns the energy of our members toward accomplishment of the vision/mission. ______

29. The church board establishes policies for finances, insurances, and personnel to protect and release the vision/mission of the church. ______

30. The church buildings adequately provide for the activities needed by a church of our size. ______

31. Pastoral leaders facilitate the life of Christ within His church. ______

32. The church works consistently to communicate and fulfill God's vision/mission in this community at this time. ______

33. A strong sense of God's supernatural presence fills our church gatherings. ______

34. Our worship services refresh our people spiritually. ______

35. The speakers at our church are good communicators of the Word of God and the vision/mission God wills for our lives and church. ______

36. Special gatherings, groups, or classes occur to assimilate newcomers, new believers, and new members into our church ______

37. Relationships are a core value in our church. ______

38. The small groups (units) in our church promote spiritual growth, accountability, fellowship, biblical application, and care. ______

39. The ministry leaders at our church build strong, effective ministries. ______

40. Our church facilitates an entrance level and advanced level of discipleship. ______

41. Our church maintains a global view of ministry, and we involve our members personally and financially in missions. ______

42. The external communications of our church give excellent visibility and result in good public relations in the community. ______

43. The leaders have created a culture of change in our church. ______

44. Our congregation supports the church with a healthy income that meets all financial responsibilities. ______

45. The physical facilities of the church reflect a standard of excellence. ______

Please identify and record your scores in the appropriate box. The number inside the boxes corresponds to each numbered statement.

| | | | | |
|---|---|---|---|---|
| 1 | 16 | 31 | Total | **Leadership** |
| 2 | 17 | 32 | Total | **Vision/Mission** |
| 3 | 18 | 33 | Total | **Spiritual Life** |
| 4 | 19 | 34 | Total | **Worship** |
| 5 | 20 | 35 | Total | **Preaching/Teaching** |
| 6 | 21 | 36 | Total | **Assimilation** |
| 7 | 22 | 37 | Total | **Care/Fellowship** |
| 8 | 23 | 38 | Total | **Small Groups** |
| 9 | 24 | 39 | Total | **Ministries** |
| 10 | 25 | 40 | Total | **Discipleship** |
| 11 | 26 | 41 | Total | **Evangelism/Missions** |
| 12 | 27 | 42 | Total | **Public Relations** |
| 13 | 28 | 43 | Total | **Decision-Making** |
| 14 | 29 | 44 | Total | **Finances** |
| 15 | 30 | 45 | Total | **Facilities** |

Allow the strength and weakness of the total scores to indicate the strength and weakness for each of the fifteen vital functions (systems) of the Church Life Model.

List the five systems with the strongest scores:

1. ______________________________

2. ______________________________

3. ______________________________

4. ______________________________

5. ______________________________

List the five systems with the weakest scores:

1. ______________________________

2. ______________________________

3. ______________________________

4. ______________________________

5. ______________________________

# APPENDIX B
# PSALM 23 PRAYER MODEL

## Psalm 23
Prayer Model

### Revelation

**Praise God for revealing Himself as...**

Verse 1) Shepherd, Guide, and Provider

Verse 2) Leader, Sustainer, and Giver of peace

Verse 3) The Restorer

Verse 4) God of the valleys and difficulties

### Request

**Ask the Lord to...**

Verse 1) Shepherd, guide, and provide for you, your family, and church

Verse 2) Lead, sustain, nourish, and give peace to you, your family, and members of this congregation

Verse 3) Bring restoration to your life, family, and the church

Verse 4) Be close as we walk through difficulty, temptation, tragedy, wounding words, and rejection

# Psalm 23
Prayer Model

## Revelation

**Praise God for revealing Himself as...**

Verse 4) Healer and Comforter

Verse 5) The Provider and Source of all things

Verse 6) Goodness, mercy, and presence

## Request

**Ask the Lord to...**

Verse 4) Comfort and heal you, your family, church members, and community

Verse 5) Provide abundantly, strengthen, and nurture us as we follow Him; give us joy

Verse 6) Give His goodness, mercy, and presence to accompany us always in this journey until we enter into His eternal home

# NOTES

## Chapter 2
## What Is the Church Life Model?

1. The term *cohort* comes from our educational experiences. My doctor of ministry group at Asbury Theological Seminary carried the term doctoral cohort. We utilized the term in the 1980's to describe our pastoral groups. Today, we also refer to the groups of pastors and leaders that we train in multiple areas of the United States as cohort groups. The Bible uses the term in Acts 10:1 to note that the centurion Cornelius belonged to a particular group of the military.
2. Kennon L. Callahan, *Twelve Keys to an Effective Church* (San Francisco: Harper Collins, 1983), xii.
3. Ibid., xii–xiii.

## Chapter 3
## What Value Does the Model Offer Local Churches?

1. Gordon D. Fee, *Paul, the Spirit, and the People of God* (Peabody, MA: Hendrickson, 1996), 45.
2. Norman Shawchuck and Roger Heuser, *Managing the Congregation* (Nashville: Abingdon, 1996), 292.

## Chapter 4
## What Are the Fifteen Vital Functions of the Church Life Model?

1. J. Robert Clinton, *Leadership Emergence Theory* (Altadena: Barnabas Resources, 1989), 72.
2. Richard Foster's *Celebration of Discipline* and *Prayer* are recommended texts for spiritual disciplines. Dallas Willard's *The Spirit of the Disciplines* remains a classic text for studies in the disciplines.
3. Christian A. Schwarz, *Natural Church Development: A Guide to Eight Essential Qualities of Healthy Churches* (Carol Stream, IL: Church Smart Resources, 1998), 31.
4. Ibid.

5. Ray S. Anderson, *The Shape of Practical Theology: Empowering Ministry With Theological Praxis* (Downers Grove, IL: InterVarsity, 1997), 62.

6. Ray S. Anderson, *The Soul of Ministry* (Louisville, KY: Westminster, 1997), 7.

7. C. Peter Wagner (ed.), Win Arn, and Elmer Towns, *Church Growth: State of the Art* (Wheaton, IL: Tyndale House, 1986), 43–45. Definitions of these stages of evangelism appear also in the glossary of terms on pp. 296 and 297.

## CHAPTER 5
## WHAT PATTERNS WORK BEST WHEN ENGAGING THE MODEL?

1. Jonathan Edwards wrote a call for corporate prayer in a work titled *A Humble Attempt to Promote the Agreement and Union of God's People Throughout the World in Extraordinary Prayer for a Revival of Religion and the Advancement of God's Kingdom on Earth, According to Scriptural Promises and Prophecies of the Last Time.* This work may be found on the Internet in many forms. It also appears in the book *A Call to United, Extraordinary Prayer* by Christian Focus Publications (2003).

2. The Reliability Analysis was performed and the report prepared by Jeffery Fulks, Ph.D., May 26, 2010. Jeffrey Fulks is the director of graduate studies at Evangel University in Springfield, Missouri.

# ABOUT THE AUTHORS

**WAYNE H. LEE** is known as "friend" and "mentor" among leaders. Following his life mission to build spiritual leaders, he has invested much of his four decades of ministry service providing resources to renew and strengthen churches, pastors, and ministry leaders. As the founder and lead consultant of Church Life Resources, L.L.C. in Lakeland, Florida, Wayne has pioneered a model and a process that brings unusual spiritual insight, clarity, in-depth assessment, health, and advancement to the local Spirit-filled church.

**SHERRY B. LEE** exhibits spiritual vitality seasoned with experience. Her multifaceted roles as educator, staff pastor, and leader of spiritual formation have served to support her life mission of empowering others for service in the kingdom of God. Sherry is the co-founder and a lead consultant of Church Life Resources, L.L.C. She and Wayne partner to create resources and train ministry leaders in the principles and process of Church Life.

# CONTACT THE AUTHORS

**WWW.CHURCHLIFERESOURCES.ORG**